Austria as It Is

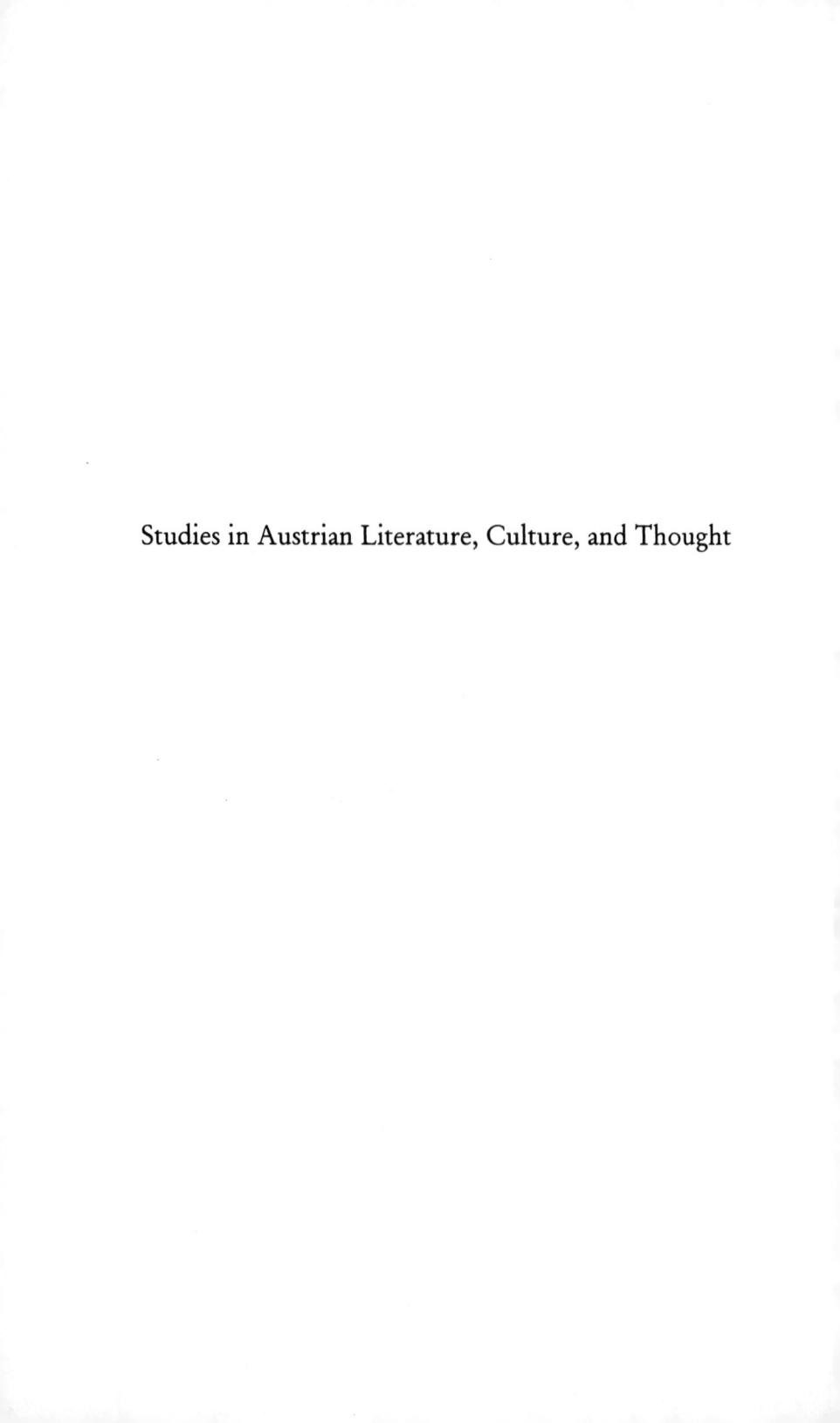

Studies in Austrian Literature, Culture, and Thought

Charles Sealsfield

Austria as It Is

or

Sketches of Continental Courts

Edited with an Introduction and Glossary
by Todd C. Hanlin

ARIADNE PRESS
Riverside, California

Library of Congress Cataloging-in-Publication Data

Sealsfield, Charles, 1793-1864.
 Austria as it is : or sketches of continental courts / Charles Sealsfield ; edited with an introduction and glossary by Todd C. Hanlin.
   p. cm.
 Originally published: London : Hurst, Chance, 1828.
 Includes bibliographical references.
 ISBN 1-57241-111-2
   1. Austria--Description and travel. 2. Vienna (Austria)--Intellectual life. 3. Metternich, Clemens Wenzel Lothar, Fürst von, 1773-1859. 4. Austria--Court and courtiers. 5. Germany--Description and travel. 6. Germany--Court and courtiers. I. Title: Sketches of continental courts. II. Hanlin, Todd C. III.Title.

DB25.S4 2003
943.6'042--cd22   2003061127

Cover
Design and Photography: Matthew Richardson
Art Director: George McGinnis

Copyright ©2004
by Ariadne Press
270 Goins Court
Riverside, CA 92507

All rights reserved.
No part of this publication may be reproduced or transmitted in any form or by any means without formal permission.
Printed in the United States of America.
ISBN 1-57241-111-2
(Paperback original)

Contents

Introduction: Carl Postl, H. Sidons, C. Sidons,
Charles Sealsfield, and Austria as It Is i

Editor's Note xvi

AUSTRIA AS IT IS: OR, SKETCHES OF
CONTINENTAL COURTS 1

Notes 110

Glossary 120

INTRODUCTION

Postl, Sidons, Sealsfield, and *Austria as It Is*

The various appellations "The New Mystery Man" and "The Great Unknown" connote several problematic aspects of the life and times of Charles Sealsfield. During his lifetime he was a mystery, an unknown in so far as his true identity was concerned; and great from the impact of his prose writings. As a young Austrian émigré, his first publications were journalistic in nature, colorful descriptions of the fledgling United States on the one hand, of the moribund Austrian Empire on the other. But within a few years he had become widely celebrated as the author of popular fiction about the American West. As the "poet of two hemispheres," he is considered the first German-American author of international significance and the originator of the ethnological novel or *Volksroman* with its regional, social, and racial variations. In his prime he was considered by many to be superior to native-American authors like James Fenimore Cooper and Washington Irving; known by some as "the German Walter Scott," the author was dubbed by Henry Wadsworth Longfellow "our favorite Sealsfield."[1]

By the age of 50, while at the height of his career and his artistic powers, he had written his last work; though he lived to be 71, he would publish no further prose fiction. At mid-century he was living in Schaffhausen, Switzerland — his stories and his values had fallen out of favor, and he was forgotten almost overnight. He returned to the United States to look after his substantial investments in railroad stocks and real estate, but became disillusioned by the absence of his favorite American ideals, by an increasing trend toward capitalism and greed, and, of course, by his disappearance from the American literary scene. Upon his return to Switzerland in 1858, he settled in the

---

[1] Alexander Ritter, "Charles Sealsfield (Karl Postl)," in *Deutsche Dichter des 19. Jahrhunderts: Ihr Leben und Werk*, 2. Auflage, Benno von Wiese, Hrsg. (Berlin: Erich Schmidt Verlag, 1979), 98.

canton of Solothurn, living a "rather lonely bachelor's existence,"[2] until his death from cancer in 1864.

One scholar has condensed his life into three phases, determined by locale: his youth in Moravia and Bohemia from 1793 to 1823; his American travels and literary career from 1823 to 1858; and his reclusive retirement in Swiss exile from 1858 to 1864.[3] The same scholar has summarized this unique life with the observation that Sealsfield represented a dichotomy, as a "poet in two regions, in two social systems, and two epochs."[4]

Karl Postl: youth, education, priesthood

Karl Anton Postl was born in the small town of Poppitz, Moravia, on March 3, 1793, to Anton and Juliana Rabl Postl. His father was a successful winegrower and local judge. Karl attended public school in Znaim, and in 1808 moved to Prague to become a student at the convent of the Order of the Holy Cross with the Red Star. Five years later, young Postl became a monk in the Order and was ordained a priest the following year. Appointed personal secretary to the Grand Master of the Order, Postl's extramural duties brought him in frequent contact with educated and well-to-do members of the upper classes within the Austrian Empire, making important connections to liberals, nationalists, and members of the Free Masons.

These formative years were greatly influenced by European and Austrian politics. The year of his birth was marked by the French Revolution, by its ideals as well as its gruesome excesses. His youth witnessed Napoleon's conquests and aspirations. And following Napoleon's dissolution of the Holy Roman Empire in 1806 with its 400-year-old Habsburg leadership, Postl's homeland was reduced to the status of a mere empire, with Francis I as Emperor. By the time

---

[2] Jeffrey L. Sammons, "Charles Sealsfield," in *Dictionary of Literary Biography*, Vol 133, James Hardin and Siegfried Mews, eds. (Detroit: Bruccoli Clark Layman, 1993), 254.

[3] Ritter, 101.

[4] Ritter, 122.

Postl had taken his vows, Napoleon had been defeated, and Waterloo was only two years off.

As Postl had sought stability in his personal life through commitment to the Order, so too did Europe hope to regain its equilibrium after the tumultuous Napoleonic years. In 1815, Postl's sovereign, Emperor Frances I, had helped form the victorious alliance against Napoleon I and thereby restored Austria as a leading European power; he now hosted the leaders of Europe at the Congress of Vienna and initiated the Holy Alliance with Russia and Prussia to maintain the status quo following the defeat of Napoleon. Francis's domestic policies also reflected his desire for continuity, discouraging liberal, nationalistic, or democratic ideals. The Austrian Prime Minister Klemens Wenzel Nepomuk Lothar, Prince of Metternich-Winneburg-Beilstein, an Austrian statesman, minister of foreign affairs from 1809 to 1848, and a champion of conservatism, was one of anti-liberalism's principal proponents and most rigorous enforcers. Through Postl's travels and personal contacts, he became sensitive to the liabilities of such repression in Bohemia, Moravia, and Hungary, among the other "Austrian" lands. Thus Francis and Metternich, as the focus of much popular dissatisfaction, also became the targets of Postl's criticism throughout his later book on Austria.

Apparently Postl became alienated from this repressive government and from the Church, due to his natural inclinations toward a more liberal and independent life. It has been suggested that as a priest he decided to break with the Catholic Church, as an Austrian with the state, and as a person with his own biography.[5] In May 1823, on official leave at a spa, Postl simply disappeared, prompting an extensive search of Moravia and Austria, but to no avail. Karl Postl had simply ceased to exist. How he escaped Austria and Austrian surveillance, how he financed his flight, and which escape route he employed are not known to this day; his biographer, Eduard Castle, makes a persuasive case for Postl's collaboration with the Free Masons, both in Europe and in the New World.[6]

---

[5] Ritter, 103.

[6] Eduard Castle, *Der große Unbekannte: Das Leben von Charles Sealsfield (Carl Postl)* (Wien: Manutius Presse, 1952), 151ff.

Postl reinvents himself

In late summer 1823 Postl surfaced in New Orleans, and for the next three years lived in Pennsylvania and New York, wintering in Louisiana. While he traveled extensively, met influential people, and perfected his English, it is uncertain what he actually did and how he earned a living during these years; he stated that he conducted business, but it is unclear exactly what that "business" entailed.[7]

Exposing himself as a true Romantic of the early 19th century, Postl championed political idealism, an adventuresome spirit, and a quest for personal freedom; this led him to shed his skin and recreate himself as a Sealsfield (sometimes misspelled by contemporary reviewers as Seatsfield, Saalsfield, Saarsfield, Searls-field)[8] — and in some few instances as a Sidons (Charles Sidons, H. Sidons, even Charles Sidons Sealsfield).

In any event, he reappeared in Europe three years later, in 1826, in possession of a bizarre passport, issued by the state of Louisiana, proclaiming the bearer to be "Charles Sealsfield, Citizen of the United States, clergyman, native of Pennsylvania." It is not known whether he was actually an ordained minister of some unnamed Protestant denomination, or whether he merely acquired the identity of a deceased American named Sealsfield.[9]

---

[7] When he returned to the U.S. in 1827 aboard the *Stephanie*, the passenger list bore the following vague but pretentious entry for a "Chas. Seafield" — "occupation: Gentleman." See Castle, 228. It is known that he later conducted certain unnamed missions and services for Joseph Bonaparte, the former King of Spain and Napoleon's older brother.

[8] See Castle, 715.

[9] Speculations regarding the source for the name "Sealsfield" range from the Englishman James Earl of Findlater and Seafield to the local Moravian vineyards *Siegelfeld* [seal-field, in German]. See footnote 1 in Gustav Winter, "Einiges Neue über Charles Sealsfield," in *Charles Sealsfield: Sämtliche Werke*, Bd. 3 (Hildesheim: Olms Presse, 1972), lxv. The other alias, "Sidons," could possibly be borrowed from the English actor (!) Henry Siddons, son of the greatest living British actress, Sarah Siddons, who is incidentally mentioned by Sealsfield in *Austria as it is*: see Winter, footnote 3, lxii.

In any event, Sealsfield insisted on maintaining his dual nationality and

Sidons as chiffre for Sealsfield

Ironically, his first attempt to gain employment made use of an identity other than that of Karl Postl. In September 1824, as "Charles Sidons," he wrote from America to the distinguished German publisher Johann Friedrich Cotta; his initial attempt to secure a position as foreign correspondent was apparently unsuccessful. In August 1826, this time as "H. Sidons," he wrote to the symbol of all that he despised in his former homeland — Metternich himself. Under this pseudonym he offered his services as an informant for the Austrian regime (a widespread practice that Sealsfield was later to criticize in his book); as a foreigner he would be of inestimable assistance in unearthing rumors, private reactions, even plots against the government. In an interview with one of Metternich's trusted diplomats, Philipp von Neumann, he then confessed that his real name was Sealsfield and that he was the American-born son of German immigrants. In this context, the appearance of a traveling American, of an independent agent without European ties, interests, or biases, must have been especially appealing to Postl. He insisted that his far-flung contacts would enable him to keep the Austrians informed as to developments in Hungary and England, two serious concerns for Metternich at the time. Von Neumann quickly became suspicious of his claims, doubted whether the foreigner could provide any useful information, and recommended that Metternich not become involved with this possible fraud. Thus when Sidon/Sealsfield was ultimately rejected, he had to look elsewhere for gainful employment; he began work on a two-volume work based on

---

identity/anonymity, as confirmed by the self-selected epitaph on his grave in Sankt Niklaus, Switzerland:
C.P
Charles Sealsfield
Bürger von
Nord Amerika
(Citizen of North America)
While still retaining his Sealsfield-alias and encrypting his true identity as Carl Postl, he nevertheless insisted on his American citizenship, while interred for all eternity in Europe.

his travels and observations in America, to be followed by yet another book, this time about his homeland, entitled *Austria as It Is*.

In 1826, Sealsfield must have been desperate for money to even consider collaborating with a scoundrel like Metternich;.[10] His detailed accounts in *Austria* of the Prime Minister's sins of omission and commission are damning; the indignation and rage expressed in these pages is clearly long-standing, and not simply a literary invention for the sake of this publication. Perhaps it is a sign of Sealsfield's grave financial state that, over the years, he would exaggerate his political connections and continually promise more than he could deliver, either as an American correspondent to important European publishers such as Cotta, or as an American informant to Metternich; he would then beg or try to wheedle an advance, with promises of producing important results.

First publications and anonymous fame

In an attempt to make a name (and an income) for himself, Sealsfield first published in London *The United States of North America as They Are in Their Political, Religious, and Social Relations*, followed by a companion piece *The Americans as They Are: Described in a Tour through the Valley of the Mississippi*; he wrote first in German, then translated both volumes into English, since he had hoped to derive income from both the German and English editions of the same works. These two volumes are journalistic in nature, part travelogue, part history, enhanced with anecdotes and folklore. They were originally intended for a German-speaking audience, not primarily as adventure tales or escapist literature, but more from the author's deeper conviction that the Old World, and particularly his Austrian homeland, could benefit from the blessings of the American experiment. An unapologetically political writer, he wrote for Europeans, against the prevailing despotism, proposing democratic

---

[10] Later, an indeterminate amount of his potential literary earnings would be siphoned off by pirate presses in France, Germany, and Scotland. See Karl J.R. Arndt, "Charles Sealsfield," in *Major Figures of Nineteenth-Century Austrian Literature*, Donald G. Daviau, ed. (Riverside, CA: Ariadne Press, 1998), 519.

principles of freedom and self-determination. Yet as one scholar has cautioned:

> Sealsfield was a man of violent and inflexible opinions.... He was an evangelist of what he presented as a revolution in the human condition that had taken place on American soil. His new Adam is a free and independent citizen; fanatically patriotic; convinced of the superiority of the American in virtue and sense to all the other servile, priest-ridden peoples of the earth; and committed to the sacredness of private property.... He reveled in the anarchism, lawlessness, and violence of American life that often worried and repelled other European observers.[11]

From the outset, the neophyte author was someone other than Karl Postl. While his first two volumes about America were written by the pseudonymous "C. Sidons, citizen of the United States of North America," all his subsequent prose fiction appeared anonymously, the ultimate attempt to conceal his identity, even as "Sealsfield" — a secret he kept until the first of his collected works appeared in 1845. Whereas the remainder of his oeuvre was published anonymously, even after he had gained fame and fortune as a successful writer, his true identity as Karl (or Carl) Postl was only discovered after his death, when his last will and testament was read and his inheritance distributed.

In 1827 he published, also in London, *Austria as It Is: or, Sketches of Continental Courts: By an Eye-Witness*, "in the guise of an imaginary travel report."[12]

Again, the combination of history and anecdote is employed to show an English-speaking readership how oppressive the Austrian regime under Francis I and his Prime Minister Metternich had become; the seditious, provocative essay was soon translated into French, German, and Spanish.

Although Sealsfield was to continue to contribute to papers and

---

[11] Sammons, 250-251.

[12] Sammons, 250.

journals as a foreign correspondent (and even edit the *Currier des États-Unis* for two years), he had effectively exhausted his book-length journalistic possibilities with both German- and English-speaking audiences. He now turned to fiction — a fortuitous inspiration, as it developed. With the publication of *Tokeah* in 1829, he enjoyed a streak of best-selling works about the American West that was to continue for more than a decade. By that time he had acquired such a reputation that a leading German literary scholar was tempted to proclaim Sealsfield "the Greatest American Author." The ensuing controversy prompted Sealsfield's publisher to issue the following statement in 1845 concerning his identity:

> The question has very often been asked "Who is Sealsfield? Could any but an American have acquired a knowledge of the manners and peculiarities of all classes in this country, as minute and perfect as that displayed in his works?" The publishers take pleasure in stating that, notwithstanding the apparent evidence to the contrary, C. Sealsfield (as his name is correctly written) was a German of singular erudition, obliged to exile himself on account of political difficulties in which he became involved. He came to this country, where he remained for several years, traveling extensively, especially through the South and West, during which time he obtained that thorough and accurate knowledge of the inhabitants of those regions which imparts such a vivid and life-like appearance to his portraiture of their characters and adventures.[13]

Austria as It Is

After completing the two volumes on *North America*, Sealsfield had wanted to write a book on developments in Hungary, but his publisher felt that there would be more interest in a book on Austria, the Emperor Francis I, and Metternich — subjects with which Sealsfield was intimately familiar. He dashed off this manuscript, and it was in print before the year was out.[14]

---

[13] As quoted by Arndt, 509-510.

[14] Castle, 220.

The book's basic premise is that this expose is written by a native European who, after a 5-year (!) hiatus in North America, returns with adequate experience and objectivity to compare the old and the new. The prodigal son disembarks at Le Havre, crosses France and several German principalities on his way to Austria; once within the borders of the Empire, he is inexorably drawn through the Bohemian countryside and Prague to Vienna, simultaneously the capital of the Empire, the seat of power, as well as the locus of all misery. The final chapters are thus devoted to life at the apex of this repressive government, with special recognition for the difficulty for Austrian writers such as Grillparzer and, by implication, himself.

While Sealsfield criticizes Government (with a capital "G") throughout the book, his greatest wrath is reserved for Emperor Francis and Prime Minister Metternich. For many years historians had viewed Francis as Metternich's puppet, yet Sealsfield innately understood the true relationship — that Metternich was merely Francis's instrument — a view that is today shared by most historians.

Sealsfield also devotes a disproportionate amount of space to his homeland, Bohemia — as a loving tribute to its people and culture, as an appeal for sympathy with its predicament under the Habsburgs, but also as a plea for support for its independence.

Austria as It Is was published in December 1827, just sixteen months after Sealsfield's arrival in Europe. While that is sufficient time to write a book of this length, it must be remembered that at some point he had written in German, and then translated into English, the two volumes about the United States. Nevertheless, the material for *Austria* was familiar to Sealsfield; the printing process was simplified by the fact that Sealsfield was no longer in London and had no opportunity to read the proofs (as evidenced by the many misspelled geographical entries and personal names of featured individuals) — in any event, a task the author frequently disdained. As one scholar has written: "beside being a far from alert copy and proof reader and no devotee to the accuracies of spelling and punctuation, he paved the way for all sorts of heedless changes by his pretense of writing in a foreign idiom."[15] Other scholars have detected even more substantial factual errors, regarding geography, history, and even observation.[16]

Did Sealsfield truly make this journey?

One intriguing question is whether Sealsfield actually made this trip. We have confirmation that he was in England, France, and Germany — indeed, the travel description from Le Havre to Frankfurt mirrors Sealsfield's actual return trip in 1826. But it is unlikely that he in fact made the remainder of the journey, with its, at times, disjointed itinerary through Bohemia. From his correspondence we know that he spent the next year-and-a-half in England, France, and Germany, wisely avoiding Austria, where he would have had to face a lengthy investigation and probable imprisonment.

Equally tantalizing is the question concerning Sealsfield's American travelling companion — whoever that might have been. Sealsfield conducts his journey in the company of "C," "my Yankee companion" from "Bucks County, Pennsylvania." In an early episode, Sealsfield describes an encounter at the border with a custom's officer:

> My friend had thought proper to place my books and writings under his immediate protection; but this precaution was almost superfluous. The custom-officer, with many bows to my companion, asked only who the other gentleman was. Being satisfied upon this point, cap in hand, he inquired after foreign books, and was going to open my trunks; when my companion signified, with a sneer, at the same time indifferent and haughty, "We will deliver the gentleman's passport ourselves. He is my friend, and you may send down to E— for a haunch of venison and a barrel of beer." The

---

[15] Otto Heller, *The Language of Charles Sealsfield: A Study in Atypical Usage* (St. Louis: Washington University, 1941), 5.

[16] Robert F. Arnold, "Die 'Tablettes Autrichiennes,' eine bibliographische Studie," in *Charles Sealsfield: Sämtliche Werke*, Bd. 3 (Hildesheim: Olms Presse, 1972), xlvi-xlix.

officer expressed his satisfaction by respectfully kissing the hand of my gracious C—....
Why would Sealsfield, as an American, need protection from another American? Why would the companion address the customs officer in English, when Sealsfield himself could have conversed with him in German? And how would the companion, a foreigner, know about E—, when Sealsfield is native to this area? These questions become more perplexing in light of the fact that, from this point in the text, the "friend" is not mentioned again; there are, at most, several references concerning a "we," but no further specific mention of "C."

Late in life Sealsfield recounted several times to his Hungarian interviewer, Karl Maria Kertbeny, that he had been accompanied by an American "diplomatic attaché"[17] — whose name Kertbeny has since forgotten. Of course, with Sealsfield's wit, another possibility arises: since the journey was imaginary, perhaps his companion was also a fictitious character, intended to enhance the author's credibility, and that the initial was possibly intended as a small joke — "C" being his current alias, "C. Sidons," or even his alter-ego and former Austrian self, "C[arl]" Postl.

Austrian Reaction

As if in ironic confirmation of Sealsfield's claims of a Metternichian police state, *Austria as it is* was immediately examined by Imperial police censors. They portrayed the book as unpatriotic, hostile propaganda, even as a danger to the state, and speculated who the author(s) might have been. They concluded that the descriptions of (Sealsfield's native) Bohemia and Moravia were extremely accurate, that the author was well-educated and probably from the upper class; he was seemingly less familiar with Vienna and with middle-class opinions. On 30 January 1828 an official report from the Court Police and Censor Office states:

These notes about Bohemia stem, as mentioned, from a very

---

[17] "Gesandschaftsattaché" — See Karl Maria Kertbeny, "Erinnerungen an Charles Sealsfield," 1864, as reproduced in *Charles Sealsfield–Karl Postl: Austria as it is: or Sketches of continental courts, by an eye-witness*, Primus-Heinz Kucher, ed. (Wien: Böhlau Verlag, 1994), 328.

observant, well-educated man, but an enemy of the government. These notes, especially the depiction of the life and circumstances of the upper nobility in Vienna, the declamations against Prince Metternich, lead us to suspect a man who belongs to the upper crust, is familiar with the circles of upper nobility and who has a special reason to hate Prince Metternich. Whether this man is himself the author or whether he provided the information to a foreigner cannot be determined.[18]

Since the book appeared in French, with publication cited in Paris and Leipzig, the Leipzig authorities were quick to search local bookstores in hopes of confiscating all available copies; this they were required to do by international treaty. Nevertheless they came up empty-handed. All of the copies sent to Leipzig had already been sold or shipped to out-of-town buyers. Thus it is evident that state censorship effectively limited the sale and distribution of the book in Austria and Germany.

Contemporary Reactions

Sealsfield and his publisher hoped to tap into a popular genre of the time, the so-called *tablettes*; this literary form, introduced by the French writer Joseph Hipployte de Santo-Domingo and copied by many others, was noted for its political indiscretion, court gossip, scandalous revelations, etc.,[19] and had developed a large and avid European readership.

Within a year, a French translation *L'Autriche telle qu'elle est ou chronique secrète de certaines cours d'Allemagne par un témoin oculaire* [Austria as it is, or the secret account of certain German courts, by an eyewitness] was on the market. By 1830, a Belgian version *Tablettes Autrichienne contenant des faits, des anecdotes et des observations sur les moeurs, les usages des Autrichiens et la chronique secrète des cours d'Allemagne par un témoin oculaire* appeared [Austrian Tablettes, containing facts, anecdotes, and observations of the manners and customs of the Austrians, and the secret account of German courts by an eye-

---

[18] *Ibid (Kucher)*, 317.

[19] Arnold, xxxix.

witness], followed four years later by a German rendition from Leipzig under the title *Seufzer aus Österreich und seinen Provinzen* [Sighs from Austria and its provinces]; the mention of further editions in Swedish and Spanish has not been confirmed. Unfortunately, the press runs of each of these editions are not known, so it is impossible to estimate how widely circulated Sealsfield's treatise actually was, by whom it was read, and thus its ultimate impact. However, a clue as to the popularity of *Austria as it is* can be seen in the "marketing" of his next work in English; though published anonymously (as was Sealsfield's practice during his literary career), it attempted to overcome the absence of author name recognition by boasting on the cover that it was written by the author of *Austria as it is*. And to judge by the number of reviews in various British, French, and American newspapers and journals, its impact must have been substantial.[20]

British critics reacted first and in greater numbers, responding to the conversational tone, the insights, the sensational revelations of this little-known Austrian Empire; the identity of the anonymous author piqued additional interest, with some critics presuming that only an educated Englishman could write so well, others correctly surmising that the author was a disaffected Austrian.

Significance of *Austria as It Is*

Though it was soon forgotten and is today considered one of the flawed early works of a major writer, *Austria as it is* occasioned an immediate response in its day: several prominent individuals at the time praised its impact on the Young Germans and others who were striving to gain political reforms, independence, cultural autonomy, or personal freedoms throughout Europe. And as a political treatise, the work is also a testimony to Sealsfield's own ideals, based on his personal experience as a citizen and democrat, accustomed to freedom and representative government. And as a journalistic prototype for the literary works to come, *Austria as it is* already explored the boundaries for the ethnological novel, or *Volksroman*,

---

[20] See Primus-Heinz Kucher, "Zur europäischen Rezeption der *Austria*, in *Charles Sealsfield–Karl Postl: Austria as it is: or Sketches of continental courts, by an eye-witness*, Primus-Heinz Kucher, ed. (Wien: Böhlau Verlag, 1994), 378.

which Sealsfield later claimed as his unique contribution to literature, with its depiction of all social classes, entire regions, their geography, history, customs and characteristics,

Critics never cease to emphasize how flawed and wretched the piece is, as Winter, for example, opines: "It truly belongs to the inferior political literature which doesn't spurn the lowest form of gossip . . . leaps about with facts, distorts the truth from time to time, and is wrong where it shouldn't be wrong."[21] Still, such a broad condemnation tends to minimize the truly unique features of this book, its variety and vitality. The skeleton of this "eyewitness" account is certainly the author's extensive knowledge of history and geography; he is able to cast his narrative in a European perspective, especially when discussing the events and repercussions of the Napoleonic Age, the Congress of Vienna, and other major historical events familiar to educated European readers. His insights into the personalities and politics of Francis, Metternich, and their underlings are also valuable in understanding the consequences for Austrians and other nationalities under their rule, for instance Bohemians and Hungarians. His political observations are supplemented and embellished by his many detailed descriptions of the fads and fancies of the age, anecdotes surrounding the major historical figures, gossip in the manner of the "chroniques scandaleuses," as well as by his dry wit — all combined to produce an eminently readable and informative essay.

To keep *Austria as It Is* in perspective, it certainly afforded four beneficial results. First, as a political pamphlet, it encouraged other Austrian subjects to continue their fight for cultural autonomy and constitutional liberty. Second, as a historical document, it provides a vivid panorama of a crucial moment in European history. Third, as a practical resource for Sealsfield, it was also intended to help make a "name" for him (whichever alias that might have been at the time) in the publishing world; here, too, it opened doors for his later journalistic career via various continental and American newspapers. Forth, and most importantly for Sealsfield, it provided the literary apprenticeship which made his later prose fiction so successful and

---

[21] Winter, lxxi [my translation]

earned for him, at least temporarily, the sobriquet "The greatest American writer."

Editor's Note

This edition of Charles Sealsfield's unique contribution to Austrian literature is not intended as a critical edition or as a photo-reproduction of the original text. Rather its purpose is to make this singular text readily accessible, once again, to its originally intended audience — an English-speaking readership. In general, I have attempted to retain the format and appearance of the original, thus preserving the flavor of this witty and provocative piece. Yet many editorial revisions were necessary. Clearly, Sealsfield did not read the pre-publication proofs, because, as an educated native-speaker of German, he would have corrected the many misspellings which appear in the text — likely a direct result of his notoriously poor handwriting.

The first significant textual error occurs on the title page: though the publication date is listed as 1828, the book was actually published in December 1827, as publication announce-ments and reviews reveal.

Many of the confusing terms in the text which required clarification are thus presented alphabetically in a Glossary of terms and names appended to the text (since Sealsfield's *Austria* is already replete with its own footnotes and endnotes). Objects familiar to Sealsfield's audience, but which are no longer in use, such as the various styles of carriages, have been glossed, along with foreign phrases. Too, within the present text, all geo-graphical references have been normalized, that is, the names of cities and towns have been given their present-day spelling to avoid confusion (e.g., Stuttgard –> Stuttgart). Spelling has also been modernized (burthens –> burdens) and Americanized (colour –> color).

Most frustrating are the proper names: there are many, many instances of proper names misspelled by the publisher (the town of Shoukof is, in reality, Schönhof; the family Testelitz should be the Festetics, to cite only two typical examples). In others cases Sealsfield himself intentionally disguised identities, only indicating individuals by elision (such as "A———ys in P——— s"). As the reader will discover, a number of the elisions are not listed here, and for several reasons: first, in some cases the individuals were either insignificant (a "face in the crowd," such as the Polish woman, the "beautiful S——," or a minor court functionary), were purposely encoded to obfuscate their identity ("B—— C——" for "Carl Breindl," for example), or were possible fictions perpetrated by Sealsfield. The intriguing question is: why would Sealsfield encode some names, especially in those cases where identification would not prove incriminating? Whatever his intention, such name-dropping clearly reinforces Sealsfield's image as an insider who knows all but who, due to noble sensitivity and discretion, does not tell all.

Sealsfield's original manuscript for *Austria as It Is* has disappeared and thus the answers to many of the above-mentioned textual questions must, like their author, remain a mystery.

AUSTRIA AS IT IS:

OR

SKETCHES

OF

CONTINENTAL COURTS

BY AN EYE-WITNESS

And yet 'tis surely neither shame nor sin
To learn the world, and those that dwell therein.
                                        GOETHE.

PREFACE.

THE Author of this work is a native of the Austrian Empire; who, after an absence of five years, has re-visited his country and found its *status quo* as exhibited in the following pages.

In presenting his work to the English public, he may be allowed to state that no person can have a more sincere respect for the just rights of monarchs, as long as they are exercised within proper bounds. But if a limited monarchy, where the three powers, legislative, judicial, and executive, are properly separated and exercised, be the most conducive to social happiness, the despotism of Austria and those kingdoms and principalities influenced by it and by the Holy Alliance, is of a nature the more shocking, inasmuch as the intellectual progress of these countries indisputably entitles them to the blessings of a liberal and rational Government. Never, perhaps, has there been exhibited an example of so complete and refined a despotism in any civilized country as in Austria.

Whether this system will bear the fruits which are expected, we doubt very much. As the Crusades of yore, to speak with Schiller,[1] which were originally intended to weaken still more the power of the princes and to extend that of the Pope in Asia, effected just the contrary and undermined his temporal dominion; so these Crusades against human liberty and understanding will, doubtless, have the same results and undermine what they are intended to strengthen — the foundation of despotism!

---

[1] See prose works of Schiller.

CONTENTS

CHAPTER I
Tour from Le Havre through France and Germany. – Paris, Karlsruhe, Stuttgart. – The late and present King of Württemberg. – Darmstadt. – Nassau. – The Elector of Hesse Kassel. – Frankfurt. Its inhabitants. – Leipzig. – Prince Poniatowski. – Dresden. – Prospect of Germany.

Page 5-15

CHAPTER II
Napoleon at Dresden. – Battles at Nollendorf and Maria Kulm. – The Austrian Police. – Teplitz. – Baths–manner using them. – Dinners. – Spies. – Promenades. – King of Prussia. – Prince Wittgenstein. – Parallel between the Prussians and Austrians. – Society at Teplitz. – Surrounding Country. – Eisenberg. – Excursion to Carlsbad. – Characteristic Features of Bohemia. – State of the Peasantry–their relation to the Government. – Character of the People. – Musical and romantic turn. – Religion.

Page 16-31

CHAPTER III
Prague. – Sitting of the Diet of Bohemia. – Nobility of Bohemia.– Private Theater of Count Clam-Gallas. – Musical Conservatorium. – Technical Institution. – Museum. – University. – The System of Education in the Austrian Empire–its consequence. – Secret Police.

Page 32-47

CHAPTER IV
Tour from Prague through Moravia and Austria. – The Empire of Great Moravia, Austria. – Vineyards. – Villages. – Inhabitants, their condition. – Church feasts. – Austrian Abbeys. – Hierarchy. – Pliability of the Clergy. – Rudolf of Habsburg and his successors.

Page 48-57

CHAPTER V
View of Vienna. – Suburbs. – Glacis. – Imperial Castle. – Imperial Apartments. – Guards. – The Emperor.

Page 58-74

CHAPTER VI
The Austrian Chancellor of State, Prince Metternich.

Page 75-82

CHAPTER VII
Austrian Aristocracy–Viennese Highlife.

Page 83-96

CHAPTER VIII
Public Officers. – Lower Classes. – The City of Vienna considered in an architectural point of view. – Public Worship. – Bias of the Viennese. – Public Institutions. – Austrian Codex. – Medical Science. – Character of its Literati. Public Journals. – Grillparzer. – Austrian Censorship. – Theaters. – Conclusive Remarks.

Page 97-109

AUSTRIA

CHAPTER I

Tour from Le Havre through France and Germany. – Paris, Karlsruhe, Stuttgart. – The late and present King of Württemberg. – Darmstadt. – Nassau. – The Elector of Hesse-Kassel. – Frankfurt. Its inhabitants. – Leipzig. – Prince Poniatowski. – Dresden. – Prospect of Germany.

LE HAVRE is not the place to dwell long in or upon. Its port is small, its entrance narrow, and in the least gale even dangerous. Its customhouse and police regulations, however, still show that its trade is flourishing, and not a day passes but some snug Yankee vessel or a heavy built French brig enters with the tide.

This town, so old in appearance, was thirty years ago a poor village inhabited by French fishermen when the discerning eye of Napoleon fixed upon it as a port for that very city, the aggrandizement of which he should least of all have encouraged. Its customhouses, police offices, cotton bales, and sugarhogsheads are not very interesting objects for a non-merchant. The third day saw me again in Rouen, to which place we ascended in the steamboat Le Havre.

The martial fierceness of the French has, since the fourteen years I last saw their country and capital, assumed a pious turn. At whatever hotel we stopped, we were sure to find prayer books and catechisms on the tables and commodes; and in Rouen we saw a large procession just entering the Gothic cathedral, joined by several dozen officers who, to our no small astonishment, hastened to this devout service with the same ardor as they did fourteen years ago to a military review. — *Sic tempora mutantur*, thought I, while my Yankee companion, whom I had offered a seat in my cabriolet, exclaimed against the pious Norman princes who, instead of cutting canals or making railroads, raised such huge, uncomfortable piles as the church at Rouen, good for nothing except catching cold: he would not exchange his meeting house for them all; meaning a wooden frame building in Bucks County, Pennsylvania.

We found in Paris an old king, more beloved however than his predecessor, notwithstanding his being surrounded with pious personages and those sprigs of the ancient nobility in whom a revolution and twenty-five years' exile could not produce the least change in their former prejudices and their notions of a golden *siècle* — the true pictures of a run down repeater, which if made to strike a hundred times will always repeat the same strokes. Of course I visited the Museum, the Tuilleries, the Palais Royal, etc. with a sort of cicerone, whose truly French pride brought honest Caleb, the worthy factotum of Ravenswood, to my mind. He commented on all the vacancies, never failing to throw the cloak of pride on the spoliations of the barbarians, as he called them: *Voilà les barbares, les Prussiens, qui ont remportés les chevaux!* — *Voilà les bêtes des Autriciens*, etc. I congratulate this nation on the good temper, or, as they term it, grace, with which they bear not only their vicissitudes, but suit themselves so exactly to the new modes with that light heart and frivolous mind which made them under Robespierre executioners, under Napoleon plundering heroes, and under Charles X pious priests. But to be serious, they have every reason to wish themselves joy. They have earned, while John Bull and poor Germany only labored. They have amassed a fine property from the spoils of other nations, and though they had to give back part of their ill-gotten fortune, their trade is flourishing; they have done away with their feudal encumbrances; and what is the chief point, they have taught their princes a lesson, which will secure, for a while, their rights better than a dozen charters. United, as they now are into one nation, they are through this union formidable; an advantage of which their neighbors, the Germans, are in want.

There is hardly any object from Paris to Strasbourg worth mentioning. Paris is almost the only town which attracts and deserves interest; the rest seem to exist only for Paris. The towns of France are generally worse than those of other countries, the villages still more so, and, except an ancient castle here and there, it is the most monotonous country imaginable.

There is in the German character a sort of familiarity which sometimes displeases, but shows at the bottom an open heart, even where there is no need of it. This, with a sincere though in a certain degree shaken attachment to their princes, constitutes one of the principal features of the present Germans. How could they else bear those incredible burdens laid upon their shoulders and which so grievously oppress them? We entered Germany on the middle of the bridge leading from Strasbourg to Baden, a fine country with a fine race of men and women, a regular capital, and a handsome palace and park. It also boasts a constitution, or, as it is termed, an assembly of states, granted by the grace of Prince Metternich. The representatives are allowed to debate how to raise the expenses for the current year, among which is a civil list of £150,000 and 10,000 soldiers. For these benefits the good people have taxes, which to pay they live on potatoes and a sort of rye bread whose color resembles exactly that of the worn-out hats we see on their heads; moreover, they are blessed with tolls and duties which, notwithstanding the Rhine washes their borders, make trade of any extent a real impossibility.

We arrived the same day in another sovereign's dominions, those of the King of Württemberg. The palace in his capital Stuttgart, is without any doubt the finest royal residence in Germany and superior to the Tuilleries in point of symmetric and architectural beauty. The crown, however, with which it is surmounted and which is not quite as large as the cupola of St. Paul's Church, seems, indeed, a satire on the royal dignity, which in this insignificant miniature kingdom is over-acted.

If wealth be dangerous in subjects, this king has nothing to apprehend. His subjects, whom we know under the appellation of Swabians, are certainly the poorest creatures in the world, and, except one wealthy bookseller, there is not a rich man in the kingdom. The present king has added to his other benefits a Diet, modified by the same princely personage, Metternich, for which his subjects are little indebted to him. He has but augmented their burdens without conferring any real benefit. The two chambers of which the assembly is composed have not the least legislative power; and their whole labor is to devise the best means of getting out of the empty pockets of the wretched subjects the taxes which the minister of the treasury imposes on the country. Among the expenses are the civil list, with £150,000 and 12,000 soldiers.

A cold shudder seizes me when I think on his late Majesty, commonly called the Fat King. He was a great huntsman. In the year 1817, during the dreadful famine, one of his deer and boar chases was held. Among the 4000 peasants who were summoned from the *Odenwald* to attend as drivers, there was a poor sick man who could not leave his bed. His only support was his daughter, who, from the earnings of her spinning, supported the miserable existence of her father. She dressed herself in her father's clothes and went to attend the royal chase. It lasted three days, during which time these people were seen *bivouacking* in snow and cold. The king heard of this disguise, laughed immoderately, and was very sorry not to have known it sooner, as it would have been an excellent joke. When the maid returned to her father's house, she found him starved. The king heard of this, but did nothing. During the same royal sport, a boar approached a peasant, when a chamberlain was just going to dart his javelin at the ferocious animal. The peasant, to defend himself, used his cudgel and prostrated the beast. The disappointed courtier now turned his javelin against the peasant, and laid him with a blow dead at his feet. As he was a favorite with the king, he came off with a fortnight's confinement.

Though the present king is rather a better sort of man, yet he is but little beloved. His travels through France, Italy, and Switzerland at the expense of his starving subjects, and his vacillating policy have changed the odium which they bore to the former into an indifference towards his successor. The beautiful royal studs of Arabian horses six miles from Stuttgart and the celebrated Dannecker's atelier at Cannstatt, are well worth a visit. In the latter, however, we find nothing, except Schiller's bust, at all worth mentioning. A tour through this kingdom is of very little interest. Miserable towns with dung hills and mud holes in the streets, houses, or rather cabins falling to pieces, still poorer villages with huts, out of whose square-foot windows wretched and fretful faces are peeping; — these are the features which accompany the traveler from Stuttgart to Heidelberg. Here the country assumes a romantic aspect, rather more friendly and prosperous, owing to the exceeding fertility of the soil and the Jew students who spend their money in the latter place. The united efforts of the German Diet at Frankfurt and of the Committee of Censors at Mainz have tamed these gentlemen in a way more galling to their feelings than even Napoleon's despotism. Half a day's ride brought us to Darmstadt, the capital of the third sovereign's dominions. Among the curiosities we found a splendid theater, an Assembly of States in the same form as that of Württemberg, 10,000 soldiers who, in the true spirit of Hessians, complain loudly of John Bull's being on friendly terms with Brother Jonathan and of being thus deprived of every chance of having their legs or arms shot off, in order to get half-pay. Another half-day's ride brought us to Frankfurt, the seat of the German Diet. A good charger may carry his rider in an hour through three sovereigns' dominions, viz: — the Elector of Hesse-Kassel, the Duke of Nassau, and the Prince Landgrave of Hesse-Homburg. A few traits, which we can state as authentic, are sufficient to give us such characteristic outlines of these princes, as may enable us to form a competent opinion of them and the respective happiness enjoyed by their subjects.

The Duke of Nassau thought proper, in the true spirit of liberality, to grant to his people a constitution. In acknowledgment for this benefit, the loyal representatives presented him with the domains of the dukedom, the national property. He accepted of the gift, passed over to Vienna, and gambled them away in the course of three successive nights. The poor people lost their only resort for paying their taxes and have now to pay their representatives who voted their property away and 6000 soldiers, besides a civil list of £100,000 to the princely family, from a country not much larger than London. His neighbor, the Elector of Hesse-Kassel, is said to be the richest, but the most despotic among the petty sovereigns of Germany; and his country is proof of it. He is indebted for his wealth to his grandfather and his father, two *worthy men*, who better than most German princes, understood the rights of sovereignty. The former proved it by selling his loyal subjects, the latter by exercising that privilege which the German princes and nobles enjoyed of yore. He left, it is said, not less than seventy-four children.

As he owed his wealth principally to his grandfather's soldiers, he paid them a proportionate attention. As soon, therefore, as he was returned to the Electorate, they had to resume their *queues*, as worn in the time of Frederick the Great. As no means could be devised in the ministerial council to fix them upon their heads, and the growth of their hair would have taken too long a time for his Highness's patience, they were fastened on their collars, to the no small amusement of the knowing students of Göttingen, who instantly provided themselves with this new headpiece, stalking with their pig tails all over the country. It happened frequently that some of the old soldiers, who followed the late elector into his exile, had still preserved their *queues* and were bound to add another, thus carrying two of these ornaments instead of one.

There is nothing more disgusting than these petty sovereigns, who, by the grace of bowing and cringing to Napoleon, became independent; a prerogative, of which they make such use as might be expected from minds narrow as their territories. They now carry on a sort of petty warfare with their tolls and duties, in that modern style which ruins a people, not at once, but by degrees. They thus contrived to make of each territory a little Japan where nothing except home growth and home produce is allowed. This combination against free trade and commerce and, in fact, against the only means of subsistence for the subjects of petty states, which have no sea coast, no produce of a superior kind, no resources, and a civil list of nearly three millions sterling, with an army of more than 100,000 men, was begun by the King of Prussia; and as every duke, or prince, or landgrave would think it derogatory to his dignity to yield to the King of Prussia in any point, they used reprisals. During my stay at Frankfurt, I had to pay for my excursion from this city into the surrounding country, a distance of three miles, not only three different tolls, but for my coachman, who carried about half-a-bushel of oats with him, a duty double the value of the oats. Owing to the same cause, a bottle of Rhine wine is, thirty miles from its growth, quite as dear as in Great Britain. What an influence such a system must necessarily produce on the brave and generous Germans, I need not observe. Poverty, smuggling with all the train of vices incident to such a policy, are the evils resulting from it. In Germany it is not the mechanic or the manufacturer, as in Great Britain or France, who is subject to periodical distress; it is the farmer, the proprietor of his estate; it is the very heart blood of the country, which is exhausted beyond any idea. There is, generally speaking, an absolute poverty — none are wealthy but the thirty-six sovereigns of this country. One may see hundreds of people and some of the most honest and industrious farmers selling their small property, which, even in

France, would support them in a decent way, and wandering to the borders of Holland to seek a foreign country; but even this sad hope is denied to them. Generally, when they arrive at the sea ports, their last penny is spent; they are refused a passage on board as redemptionaries; and they either starve or return absolute beggars. It is truly wonderful how the princes of Germany could have allowed liberty a little nook in Frankfurt, the very heart of the country, and where the effects of this freedom are so strangely contrasted with the surrounding poverty. We may account, however, for this phenomenon by a sufficient knowledge of the character of their subjects. A newly-discovered Minnelied,[2] such as the Nibelungen (N-1)[3] will make them forget constitution, liberty, and misery; and though they can exactly tell what sort of Government China, Japan, and Siam have, and give an exact account of the mismanagement in these empires, yet it never occurred to them that their own is the very worst of all.

Frankfurt is an ancient and noble city, where a proportionate wealth is diffused through all the classes of society, though their liberty is rather galled by the overweening airs of the Austrian and Prussian sinecure ambassadors.(N-2) It is the only city in the south of Germany which, besides Vienna, may be said to be rich; and though the greatest part of these riches is in the hands of half-a-dozen Jews, yet they share the spoils, which flow into the gulf of Hebrew subtlety from the sweat of the brows of the Austrian, Prussian, and Russian slaves. It is a pity that the high character of the Germans and their virtues are so little known, and still less esteemed. There is an intenseness of feeling in the German character, which touches the very heart.(N-3)

To an incredible extent of knowledge and enlightened learning they unite an unostentatious simplicity and unassuming manners, which bespeak the sterling cast of their minds. What would this

---

[2] Love lays

[3] Numbers preceded by N in parentheses denote endnotes. See page 124ff.

nation become, were they allowed only a small degree of civil liberty? A social circle of the better class in Frankfurt has a particular charm. Out of fifteen young ladies and as many gentlemen who meet in a company, there will scarcely be five who are not versed in English literature; and Walter Scott, Moore, and Cowper are their favorites. The salutations and unshawlings are scarcely over, when the knitting work is resorted to; while one or two are playing on the pianoforte or reading a favorite novel of the above-mentioned authors. They are interrupted by the tea party, after which they hasten to the Cecilia Union, an institution highly honorable to the youth of Frankfurt. About fifty young ladies of the best families, with as many gentlemen, assemble regularly twice every week, to perform Handel's, Haydn's, Grauns's, etc. classical works under the direction of a musical gentleman of high standing. The salary of this director (Shelble), the expenses of the *locale* and of the orchestra are defrayed by subscription of the members. Only sacred music is here admitted. I heard the *Messiah* and Haydn's *Creation* performed, and I do not hesitate to affirm, that although the London performance is more splendid as relates to the orchestra, yet the general impression produced by these hundred youthful and blooming singers is far superior to anything I ever heard.

The tower where the emperors of Germany were crowned is interesting, if it were but to convey an adequate idea of the ancient notions of magnificence. The hall where the coronation took place is an oblong chamber or rather a chapel, such as we find in moderate country mansions of Great Britain. The worn-out likenesses of the emperors, the more ancient of whom have visibly been renovated at various times, and the scene of desolation which reigns throughout are true representations of the present state of the Holy Roman Empire.

The country between Frankfurt and Leipzig, if we except the Fichtel mountains and a dozen small residences of Saxon princes, is of little interest. We visited at Leipzig the spot where the gallant Poniatowski fell, the hope and the idol of his countrymen. Fanciful and enthusiastic as they are, it was no wonder they once clung with fondness to the hope of seeing him seated on the throne of the Sobieskis and Casimirs.(N-4) A very curious circumstance respecting the fate of this interesting prince, and one authenticated by several of his friends, is the following: he was, about six years before his death, on a visit to a relation of his in Silesia with a numerous party. They were assembled in the pavilion of the country seat, when a plaintive but melodious voice was heard before the gate. It came from a gypsy, who was called in to prophesy the fate of each person. The first who stepped forth was Prince Poniatowski. The gypsy took his hand, looked attentively at it, then at him, and muttered in a low voice, "Prince, an Elster will bring you death." As Elster in the German language denotes both the river Elster and a magpie, the company made merry, wrote the prophecy down, witnessed and sealed it. It is still extant.

The prosperity of Saxony, notwithstanding the ravages of a war which led a million of soldiers at different times into the heart of the country, and the subsequent division or rather laceration of this little kingdom seems but little affected. The healing hand of a paternal Government is everywhere visible. Whatever may be the fault of the king, whose plain honesty and ill-timed faith led him to persevere in an alliance when his royal and princely brethren and cousins were already playing false, he has severely suffered; but even in his sufferings, this venerable patriarch of kings is an instance of what common sense with true honesty may perform in so short a time. His simple method was that which every wise father of a family, whose speculation proved fatal, resorts to — retrenchment of his expenses and a strict honesty in fulfilling his obligations. This honesty has effected what no other aggrandized monarch can boast of: a firm public credit, prosperity, a trade but little diminished, security, and an unbounded love of his subjects. The inhabitants of Dresden and of Saxony in general are renowned for their good manners, cultivated taste, and frugality. A dozen well-dressed gentlemen will sit down in the first hotels to dinner, which consists of a wing of a fowl and two thin slices of bread and butter — a very moderate lunch for an Englishman. This frugality may originate in a comparatively poor soil, which yields its tribute not without hard labor; but it is certainly a high commendation for their princes, that they have opened to their subjects sources of mental perfection in those well-known treasures of the gallery, which justly give Dresden the appellation of the Florence of Germany. Compared to this gallery, the treasures of the Green Vault are mere trifles. You stand hours and days before the

Madonna without being satiated and always return from your rambles into the adjoining rooms to this *ne plus ultra* of genial art.

Dresden has no splendid edifices; even the Catholic church, the palace of the king, and that of Count Marcolini are not imposing; but the whole city presents so beautiful an *ensemble* — its situation, without being romantic, is so calm; the bridge, built in a chaste and noble style and with such perfect propriety, spans both towns — that the impression which it leaves behind is certainly a most pleasing one. If we add to this the absolute gentleness of their literary character, some of whom are of a distinguished standing, as Böttiger and Nostiz, one is indeed sorry to leave a city where so much taste and refinement are blended with the most unassuming manners.

Will Germany, after having had its Müllers, Fichtes, Herders, Schillers, Goethes, etc. follow the course of human nature and establish a national liberty, such as is the inseparable companion of a free will, the result of an enlightened understanding? Will it follow the example of England, which resumed its natural rights when its Shakspeares, Addisons, and Miltons had diffused light through the ranks of their countrymen; or the example of France, after its Corneilles, Racines, Montesquieus, and Rousseaus had done away with the prejudices of a feudal and barbarian age?

Divided as Germany is into petty districts, separated from each other by jealousies, manners, and many antiquated prejudices, but, above all, governed by princes who, devoid of every national character, are the tools of Austria and Prussia, as they formerly were of Bonaparte; by the united efforts of these powers and princes, and the *"reign of darkness,"* the Germans will gradually sink into that state of slavery fit to become subjects for Russia, when this power shall have subdued Austria and Turkey, and have annexed to its empire Bohemia, Moravia, the rest of Poland, and Hungary. The genius of culture draws towards the West. It rose in the beautiful plains of Euphrates, Tigris, Araks, and Ganges. They are now a desert. It moved towards the borders of the Mediterranean, and Lydia and Ephesus shone forth. Their glory is gone too, to make place for the bright star of beautiful Greece, whose splendor sunk with the walls of Corinth, and Imperial Rome took the command of the world. She is now only extant in the records of history, and Europe's hope rests on the proud rock of Albion. But the tide runs towards America, and, perhaps, before two centuries shall have elapsed, the genius of Europe, to avoid Scythian fetters, will have alighted on the banks of the mighty Mississippi.

May the genius of Europe never fly from this noble, proud, and happy Island! May it forever be what it has shown itself — the bulwark of liberty!

CHAPTER II

Napoleon at Dresden. – Battles at Nollendorf and Maria Kulm. – The Austrian Police. – Teplitz. – Baths, manner of using them. – Dinners. – Spies. – Promenades. – King of Prussia. – Prince Wittgenstein. – Parallel between the Prussians and Austrians. – Society at Teplitz. – Surrounding Country. – Eisenberg. – Excursion to Carlsbad. – Characteristic Features of Bohemia. – State of the Peasantry, their relation to the Government. – Character of the People. – Musical and romantic turn. – Religion.

WE set out from Dresden on our way towards the Bohemian frontier on the same road which saw, fourteen year ago, the Austrian, Russian, and Prussian eagles fleeing from the great Corsican. It was the last great scene of his victorious life. Two days of uninterrupted attacks during a flood of rains had left him victorious on the field of battle; and when he returned to the city, tired and worn out, the flaps of his three-cornered hat bending downwards, the water running in streams out of his boots and clothes, the inhabitants of Dresden, struck with the greatness of his exertions, broke out into shouts of *"Vive l'Empereur!"* which touched the conqueror to the very heart. With a tear in his eye, a thing seldom to be seen, he remarked to Berthier, *"Voilà des acclamations qui sont sincères;"* and instantly turning aside and letting the 7000 Austrian prisoners, taken in this battle, pass by, his features darkened, and a gloom spread over his face which never left him afterwards: it was the gloom of rage and revenge. He then perceived that the alliance formed at Prague was of another sort and that his enemies were determined to destroy him. His character solves the question why he rejected a peace offered him under very favorable terms. It was rage, the desire of vengeance, of humbling, and perhaps finally exterminating that very sovereign whom he despised, and who had now outwitted him. A mind like his, powerful and stern, grown up under military discipline, not smoothed nor softened in the refined circles of high life; accustomed to command, but not to yield with grace, could not brook to seek peace from those whom he formerly had in his power. He felt only the enormous treachery of Austria; and as an enraged fencer who, though possessed of a superior force, is met by a less able but cool-blooded antagonist, will lay open his side, he rushed on with that impetuosity which laid the first foundation of his ruin. The first battle after that of Dresden plainly confirmed this. His whole rancor fell on Austria: and, to satisfy his thirst of vengeance, he sent into the intricate defiles of Bohemia an army under his most cruel but least expert general, the well-known Vandamme.

We passed over the same road from Peterswalde to Nollendorf. A "Halt!" interrupted my conversation with my companion and reminded us where we were. A black and yellow-painted beam, which crossed the whole road, was in the act of being lowered so as to preclude our passage. A custom officer, with a sergeant and two soldiers, stepped out of a door surmounted with the double eagle. My friend had thought proper to place my books and writings under his immediate protection; but this precaution was almost superfluous. The custom officer, with many bows to my companion, asked only who the other gentleman was. Being satisfied upon this point, cap in hand, he inquired after foreign books and was going to open my trunks; when my companion signified with a sneer, at the same time indifferent and haughty, "We will deliver the gentleman's passport ourselves. He is my friend, and you may send down to E——— for a haunch of venison and a barrel of beer." The officer expressed his satisfaction by respectfully kissing the hand of my gracious C———, the soldiers by a grim smile; and we rolled down the defiles of Nollendorf, famous for the resistance which 3000 Prussians under their general, Kleist, surnamed Count de Nollendorf, offered here to the pursuing Vandamme, till a sufficient force was collected in the rear. The road descends into a deep ravine, surrounded on three sides with huge mountains, whose forest-clad cliffs witnessed fourteen years ago the bloody and desperate contest, known under the name of the battle of Maria Kulm. The valley opens here towards the south. The principal conflict was on an eminence, defended by the Russian guards under Ostermann. The Prussians were on the right, the Austrians on the left side. The French fought with an assurance not yet dismayed by disasters, the Allies with despair. The battle was decided in favor of the latter by the arrival of the Austrian general

Colloredo, and 9000 Frenchmen surrendered; 4000 escaped; the rest of the army, 40,000 strong, were killed, wounded, or dispersed. Two monuments, the one erected by the King of Prussia to the memory of the fallen Prussians, the other by the Bohemian nobility to their countryman, Count Colloredo-Mansfeld, who died in 1824, commemorate the names of the leaders.

St. Maria Kulm is the first nobleman's seat which, on entering from this side, offers itself to our view, — an elegant mansion in modern style, surrounded with parks, gardens, and a number of dwellings for the household officers, at a short distance from the borough of St. Maria Kulm. The noble proprietor is a Count Thun. We thence rode in one hour and a half to Teplitz, the celebrated Temple of Hygæia for all those numerous disorders produced by a too free indulgence in the gifts of Ceres, Bacchus, and Venus.

The town is just built in that accommodating style, which leaves it entirely at your choice whether you will spend with the King of Prussia £5 a day or one shilling. Your appearance and resources are the standard of the behavior of the dreaded police, when you have to send or to deliver your passports.

A foreigner who comes to Austria from a distant country and bears the truth of his statement in his appearance and resources will have less reason to complain of the police than in France or Prussia. Its dead weight lies chiefly on the people. The higher classes, even among foreigners, are allowed more liberty, and, if they are not stigmatized as *revolutionaires*, they are here more at their ease than anywhere else: certainly much more than in Prussia. There are, however, two things which I advise John Bull not to overlook. When an absentee from his country, he is inclined to adopt the saving principle: now, for my part, I have not the least objection to his retrieving his circumstances by a voluntary exile; but then it becomes him, even for his own good, not to show contempt or disrespect towards that nation, be it what it may, where he is going to retrieve his fortune; the more so, as this very principle of saving in a foreign country, in order to be enabled to spend more at home, is in itself an affront to the country he visits. A second thing is to guard his tongue. Freedom is a diamond which sparkles in England and ought to be the more prized for its rarity. Show your diamond to robbers or paupers, and they will either rob you or despise the possession of what they cannot duly appreciate: — show your freedom to slaves and their taskmasters, and you may incur still more serious consequences.

The town of Teplitz is very elegant: the houses, which are numerous, are clean and solid; some are very handsome: the palace of the Prince Clary, the proprietor of Teplitz, though not of superior architecture, has an imposing effect. Besides several private bathing places, there are the town baths, those of Prince Clary, and of the King of Prussia. They are either of marble or of a white stone and kept very clean. The water, before it is used, is exposed for ten hours to the open air, in order to cool; but, notwithstanding this, the heat is so great that, on entering the bath, you are scarcely able to support it. For the indigent, two large reservoirs are appropriated, where males and females bathe separately. They receive, besides, every day a small sum of money towards their support. The efficaciousness of these baths is admitted to be superior to those of Aix-la-Chapelle and Wiesbaden: the regulations are conducted with a propriety nowhere else to be met with. The use of a bath is generally followed by a *siesta* of an hour; after which breakfast and then a short walk is taken. At three o'clock dinner is served in the great garden salon. One of your neighbors is perhaps a Bohemian nobleman, the other a Russian, the third a Pole. From their safeguards, posted with a *serviette* and a plate behind their chairs, and from their hangers, broad silver or gold epaulettes, you might mistake them for Prussian or Russian generals, if their obsequious smile did not declare the contrary. The company there consists entirely of nobility; and you know at once where you are and feel at home without those embarrassments which fall so often to your lot in a German refreshing place, where, on the right side, you have a prince perhaps with £500 a year; on your left, a Prussian ensign, which makes you return the cordiality of the former with a cold silence, and the *sabreure arrogance* of the latter with an obsequious smile. A concert, such as you hear only in Bohemia, not numerous in performers, but harmonious with its fine concords, for which this nation is so celebrated, thrills through your very soul and makes you forget deer haunches, bear hams, and Bohemian pheasants — articles which even Napoleon acknowledged so superior that annually 500 braces of them made the tour to Paris. A profusion of Rhine, Champagne, and, above all, of Hungarian wine covers the table; for we must do justice to the liberality of the Austrian

Government, which, if it circumscribes your spiritual, pays the more attention to your physical concerns and allows you what no other Government would do, to import as much foreign wine as is thought sufficient for your wants. The conversation during dinner turns on anything but politics. The Russian will talk about the last Hungarian vintage; the fat Austrian general about the flavor of the pheasant; and the Pole speaks to none but his fair countrywomen, who occupy the head of the table. One of these persons, however, deserves your attention. He has a smiling face, speaks fluently French, English, and German — a sort of weathercock, of whose character you are quite uncertain; but if you are a newcomer you may be sure of having him *vis-a-vis* at the table. While the Russian count treats him with a great deal of civility, the Pole darts furious looks at him; the Austrian general looks up to him with a sort of humility, and his aide-de-camp, the young, rich Count N———, treats him decidedly *en bagatelle;* but this personage is quite unconcerned. He is a close observer; and, if you are a stranger, you may be sure of being attentively watched. He is the counselor of the Bohemian Government, B——— C———, the Imperial spy who, at the expense of his Majesty, spends the season here and lives in very high style, known to every body in the company, on familiar terms with all, and terrible to none except to the unwary. You will find this personage everywhere, even in the private circles of the nobility; for, in order to show their loyalty and how "*hand and glove*" they are with the Imperial interest, they think it necessary to have the good opinion of B——— C——— or of his colleagues in other bathing places.

After dinner, at five o'clock, you are invited to take a tour to one of the surrounding villages if the weather is fine, if not, to the park of Prince Clary. Two large basins with half-a-dozen swans, clumps of the finest limes, and all sorts of forest trees with underwood exhibit the pure English taste of the noble proprietor. There you meet every day, and braving every weather, two persons: the first, a lank, tall figure without proportion, striding with paces two yards long; a face sullen and gloomy — his companion, a thin-legged little man, bespattered from head to foot with mud, and kept in a constant *career* by his mighty foreman. It is the King of Prussia, who never fails to take, after or during rain, these pedestrian exercises, to the no small discomfort of his little attendant, the grand chamberlain Prince

Wittgenstein, who follows, or rather runs after his royal master, breathless, through thick and thin. During this excursion not a single word is spoken. The sovereign probably meditates on some great improvement in the appearance of his soldiers. It is not two weeks since he sent an express from here to Berlin with orders to change the black sword knots of his soldiers into white. The speed of the courier excited considerable alarm, not only here, but in Vienna; but in eight days the important secret was manifest. These improvements and *Choco* in Paris are said to be his principal pleasures. About four weeks ago, and previous to his departure from Berlin, an occurrence took place which alarmed his Majesty not a little. He was walking in the park at some distance from the Royal Palace. A man with his right hand in his bosom approached him; the King, terror-struck, and thinking on Sand, turned and retreated with hasty strides towards the palace, the man following him. The King arrives, running and breathless, at the entrance of his residence, where he gives an order to arrest and examine the pursuer: trembling, he retires to his apartments, when the Crown Prince rushes in, his hand in his bosom, and, extracting a petition, exclaims, "Here is the dagger which was intended for your life!"

The crestfallen monarch read the petition, ordered his son to be placed under arrest, and dismissed the supplication. Following their rival master, the Prussian visitors keep separate, or rather are kept separate, from the other guests: it is not a loss to society. There is but one voice respecting the insufferable arrogance of these *sabreurs*. Between them and the Austrians, and especially their military men, there subsists a bitter jealousy; the Prussians never failing to assume an air of superiority, which to a foreigner is ridiculous, as they generally make a very poor appearance, and there is little reason with either for being overly proud. They are both slaves; the one to the military whims of a gloomy king, the other to a smooth-tongued prime minister. As for their respective military glory, the Prussians, it is true, gained victories under their great Frederick, but under such a leader any troops might have proved victorious. During the war of 1790-1794, they proved very indifferent soldiers, and during the period of 1806 they dared not even face the French. On the other hand, Austria continued a warfare of twenty-five years, not without honor; and, though often beaten, her armies have regained their reputation and defeated Napoleon when in the height of his power, in the certainly glorious battles of Aspern and of Wagram. As for the last war of 1813-1814, Napoleon succumbed to numbers, having lost the assistance of Austria. Frederick William III would else be planting Indian corn in some part of the United States, and his shrewd son, instead of broaching his wit on his father and the guards, would be clearing fields, as other honest Yankees do.

Teplitz has charms, as you will find. The whole is regulated on a noble footing. There is no trace of that venality and beggar-like obtrusion, so disgusting in German refreshing places. At your departure, you pay the orchestra a small sum for the delicious table music you enjoyed, without being in the least troubled by those ambulatory musicians who oblige you to keep your hand always in your pocket, and to carry with you the *kreutzers* and *groschens*, and those nameless sorts of bad coinage for which Germany is so celebrated. The Austrian police has at least one good feature — it is the close attention which it pays not only to the comfort, but even to the inexperience of the sojourner. Landlords, hackney coachmen, and all that train of hangers-on infesting baths and hotels are here honest from necessity. An extorting landlord is fined without mercy, and footmen are ordered away, should they dare to impose on a sojourner.

The female society of the high class consists mostly of Russian, Saxon, and Polish ladies. More captivating and more dangerous than a Polish lady nothing scarcely can be conceived. His late Majesty, the Emperor of all the Russias, made a sad experiment even with the aunt of the two most beautiful creatures who adorned, during my stay, the circles of Teplitz. The subscription paid in 1811, for a year, to the P———ss M———y exhausted his Imperial Majesty so completely, that, a few gallantries with the late Q———n of his P———n M———y excepted, his Imperial consort had afterwards very little reason for jealousy.

Are you fond of beer, smoking, and military exploits, repeated a hundred times? Then seek the company of Prussians, and you may have a can of beer administered at the Eagle or the Wild Boar; the battles of Katzbach and of Bar-sur-Aube and Montmartre; and hear how Wellington with his whole army would have been cut to pieces, had it not been for their arrival. And, to remove all doubt, they will show you, out of a pocket book which had once been red, the plans of these battles.

The country about Teplitz is called the Paradise of Bohemia and is the focus of Bohemian high life during the summer months. Several dukes, princes, and a number of counts spend the summer here at their castles and their country mansions, many of which are equal, if not superior, to the finest country seats in England. The most beautiful are the castles of Eisenberg, Postelberg, Rothenhaus, Schönhof, but above all Raudnitz. The immense estates of the nobility preclude those variegated scenes, those innumerable beautiful forms, embellished by an exquisite sense of rural beauty, those trim hedges and lawns and grass plots, watered by the hand of Nature, the delightful features of an English landscape. You behold beautiful villages buried, as it were, under forests of fruit trees; here and there a superb castle rising over the humble cottages, and surrounded by extensive parks, seldom trodden by a human foot, except that of the ranger. Our first excursion was to Eisenberg, belonging, with the domain of the same name, to the Prince of Lobkowitz. After having passed a forest for three miles, the castle presented itself almost perpendicularly over our heads. Three avenues, hewn into the forest, lead up to the open foreground on the summit of the highest mountain in the surrounding country. From the midst of it this superb mansion rises lofty and commanding in the form of a sexagon of three stories, whose pavilions are surmounted with cupolas. A herd of deer, after having stared a while at the approaching carriage, lost themselves in the gloomy forest. Two balconies, resting on Ionic pillars, decorate the front and the entrance. From the lobby, decorated with columns of the same order, you ascend a flight of stairs which leads from both sides to the first story. It is exclusively for the prince and his family. The picture of one of his ancestors, Bohuslaus de Lobkowitz, from the pencil of Skreta, decorates the great salon. The rooms are throughout furnished in a princely style. The second story is for strangers, who, even during the absence of the prince, are received and entertained in a most hospitable manner. We accepted the invitation of the castellan to stay there for a day; but declined the invitation to attend the deer chase, which was to be given a week afterwards in honor of the prince's arrival. These deer chases are rather a tame pleasure in Bohemia; it is merely driving ten or fifteen bucks to the outskirts of a wood, where the sportsmen are stationed. They are shot, or rather slaughtered, as they approach. A dinner and a ball conclude the entertainment. The view from this castle is truly grand. On the northeast, there towers into the clouds, which rising and lowering seem still to be influenced by the magic powers of Rübezahl, the king of the Sudites, the Schneekoppe; to the west, the Saxon Erzgebirge; and to the south, the beautiful Bohemia with its infinite variety of ruins, castles, towns, villages, spread like a carpet before your eyes. This castle is visited once every year by the prince and his family for a month or two during the sporting season. The forests belonging to this domain amount to 100,000 acres, part of which is inclosed, and stocked with 250 deer and fifty boars. Every third year a deer hunt is held, which is attended by the nobility and surrounding country. This establishment, which in England would require at least £2000 a year, is here carried on with comparatively very little expense. The game is supplied with barley from the ten farms of the domain, containing about 25,000 acres of arable land, meadow, orchards, and hop gardens. They are so situated as to be surrounded by the sixty villages which appertain to this estate, the inhabitants of which are bound to perform the menial duties, plowing, keeping the roads in order or laying out new ones,, and to attend the field sports, which are held regularly on these farms and the lands of the peasantry. The economy of the domain is superintended by a director, the forests by an inspector: both are responsible to the Government; the first, for the execution of the Government's orders, which he carries into effect; the second, for the proper management of the forests.

The revenues of this vast domain are raised from the produce of the fields, and iron furnaces, the sales of timber, the tithes of the subjects, and the taxes which they have to pay from sales of their property to their lord. The clear income amounts to £45,000 which, with six other domains and his dukedom, (Laudwitz), yield a clear revenue of from £20,000 to £25,000 – a sum sufficient in Austria to keep up the highest style. There are in Bohemia, comparatively, but a small number of freeholders possessed of estates. Almost all the proprietors of lands are either dominical, viz. possessors of domains, or rustic subjects of these domains. Of course, the landed nobility of Bohemia still exercise a considerable influence over their subjects, far greater than in Austria proper. The Government feels the necessity of cajoling them, relaxing or resuming its rigor, just as the public spirit seems to require. We returned two days afterwards and took the road through Brüx, an old town with a stock sufficient to provide the whole kingdom of Bohemia with its namesake. The use made hitherto of these treasures is very limited; everyone digs for bricks on his lands, just as he thinks proper.

One of the most interesting spots in Bohemia, and we may say in the world, is Carlsbad. The road from Teplitz to Carlsbad leads through an expanse of wheat fields, forty miles in length, without the least interruption. It is the richest and most fertile part of this kingdom. The peasants are generally wealthy. Between the towns Saaz and Komotau lie the superb castle and the domain of Prince Schwarzenberg, celebrated for sports. Twelve thousand head of game (pheasants and hares) fall annual victims to these sports, to which the surrounding nobility and gentry are either invited or admitted. Carlsbad lies at the outskirts of the Erzgebirge. We arrived the morning of the second day, after a tour of fifty-eight miles, at a platform from which a road winds along the ridge of a mountain, 1800 feet high, into a deep valley. The town is now horizontally at your feet and again moved from your sight by the windings of the *chaussée*. Arches, from thirty to fifty feet high, rise from the declivities and support the *chaussée;* a magnificent specimen of modern architecture, which, for boldness and solidity, is superior to everything of this kind on the continent. The carriage rolls down with ease, without having its wheels locked; and you arrive in the town unconscious of the tremendous height, till you look up from the abyss. Carlsbad extends for about a mile in a valley, from a quarter to half a mile in width, watered by the small river Tepl. Close behind the houses, the mountains rise like mighty walls in precipitous and wild magnificence. In the midst of this pretty little town with about 300 houses, just before the stone bridge, the Sprudel pours forth its boiling waters. It is covered with a rotunda, where you behold fashionables of almost every nation sipping and scalding their lips with the boiling waters of this celebrated fountain. You cross the stone bridge, and a narrow street leads you to the Neubrunnen, the water of which is generally resorted to by the newcomers, who, after every bumper, stride with hasty paces along the wooden gallery running along the bank of the

Tepl. Generally they begin with eight glasses, taken at intervals of a quarter of an hour, advancing to sixteen, and even to twenty-four, four of which, in the last stage of the cure, are taken from the Sprudel.

It is the resort of all the hypochondriacs, splenetics, misanthropes, and *sedentaries* of all descriptions. Nature seems to have chosen this place for those mental patients who wish to forget the wounds inflicted in the storms of society. Its inhabitants are gifted with that cheerful and alleviating temper which exists only for the comfort of their visitors. The narrow space, in which this beautiful little town is compressed, reduces the 2000 inhabitants and as many visitors to a single family; and you can be hardly two days here before everyone will know you. The natives, like their visitors, are quite the reverse of those of Teplitz — a gay, lively race, indefatigable to make their guests comfortable during the season. They are said to make amends for their trouble, during the winter, when they regularly spend the earnings of the summer. And while the fashionables of Teplitz are confined in the morning to their beds, those of Carlsbad are seen crowding near the two fountains and digesting, by mighty strides, the regular prescription. A carriage, that indispensable requisite in Teplitz, is seldom seen in these narrow streets, unless it be for an excursion to Eger, to pay a visit to the manes of Waldstein, the victim of his superstition and ambition. Most visitors prefer sauntering through the beautiful and shadowy promenades; or climbing, in every direction, the precipitous cliffs to Lord Findlater's temple. The regular sedentaries pace quietly through the park, which extends on the upper end towards the Hammer. The effective powers of these waters are too well known to require explanation. They were discovered by Charles IV, who, pursuing a deer and on the point of discharging his arrow, saw the animal plunge into a well, from which arose columns of steam. His attendants would fain have persuaded him that it was the kitchen of some magician: the undaunted and, for his age, enlightened monarch explored it and thus bestowed one of the greatest blessings on all the heroes of the quill, from the prime minister down to the poor author who, as he blesses this delightful spot, remembers, not without shuddering, the Congress of Carlsbad.

We returned, highly satisfied with our excursion, on the same road to Teplitz. The best mode of traveling in Austria is in your own carriage with post horses: the fixed price for two horses is seven shillings for ten miles. As carriages may be had at a very easy rate, this manner of traveling is generally resorted to, and only the inferior classes are seen crowding into the stages or, as they are called here, the diligences. The road from Teplitz to Prague, seventy-six miles, lies through Lobositz, Gitschin, and Wellwan. A trip of a few miles will carry you thence to the magnificent summer residence of Prince Lobkowitz, Duke of Raudnitz. This is one of the finest domains in Bohemia: the castle and parks are on the grandest scale, the latter stocked with 400 deer and boars. This, with the picturesque scenery of the surrounding country, the vine-covered mountains of Melnik, its decaying castle, and the lordly Elbe give to the scenery an air of inexpressible grandeur and sadness. The whole country exhibits a sort of still life, which contrasts in a strange manner with the beautiful variety of the scenery, and still more so with the deep and intense character of its inhabitants. The vineyards near Lobositz and Aussig and those of Melnik and Raudnitz, laid out and planted with scions from Burgundy under Charles IV, are still vineyards. The villages are confined to their narrow boundaries as they existed 200 years ago. The towns through which we passed, Budin and Leitmeritz, are in tolerable order and even superior to those of an equal size in Germany; but as the decaying walls show scarcely their bounds, a new house has been added. There is, indeed, between Budin and Leitmeritz the strong fortress Maria Theresienstadt, garrisoned in time of war with 1200 men; but this is, of course, no benefit for the country. The houses of the Bohemian peasantry are generally built of stone or bricks dried in the sun; and thatched with straw or with shingles; those of the wealthier with tiles: only the floor of the principal room is boarded.

The Austrian Government, afraid in any manner, from its peculiar situation, of raising the spirit of its subjects, which might endanger their trammels, allows them to prosper only just as much as will enable them to eat, to drink, to pay taxes, and to have a few guldens in case of a war. Store is not thought of, or rather it is presumed dangerous. It is a curious circumstance, that the emperor only gave his consent to the famous national bankruptcy, when his minister Wallis represented to him that the excessive abundance of the currency had raised the spirit and the enterprise of his subjects so as to endanger their subjection. On the other hand, if the farmer is not able to pay his taxes, as is really now the case with 1000 of them, not only a respite, but even a remittance is allowed them, and their farms are seldom or never publicly sold.

The Bohemian peasantry enjoy a certain degree of freedom: they are not the property of their lords, as in Hungary; they may marry and sell their estates, but are not allowed to buy a lordship as a domain. From their estates they have to pay double the taxes, in proportion to an equal number of acres possessed by their lords; besides tithes to their lords and their parsons, and the performance of menial offices, either for their families, or, if they are possessed of a team, with their horses and cattle. These menial offices are regulated by the Supreme Agrarian Aulic Tribunal, under the superintendence of the Committee of the States of the kingdom. The medium through which they are carried into execution is the director with his subalterns, a comptroller, a secretary, clerks, and beadles. These officers are salaried by him and subject to the proprietor of the domain, but they are, at the same time, answerable to the Government. The director collects and delivers the taxes to the chief town of the circle. He is the means of carrying into effect the conscription, of laying out public roads, raising provisions for the army, and directing public measures in regard to the peasantry. He constitutes the immediate or first political tribunal to which the peasant applies. In case he abuses his power, the peasant is allowed to appeal to the second and higher tribunal, the captain of the circle,[4] who holds the rank of counselor of the government or colonel of a regiment, resides in the chief town of the circle, and has four commissaries with a number of clerks. The third tribunal to which a peasant may resort is the Government of the kingdom, headed by the Supreme Burggrave as president, who has under him a vice president and thirty counselors. The fourth tribunal to which a peasant has access is the *Aulic Chancellery*, under the immediate direction of the Minister of the Interior; the last, the Emperor with his State Council, of which he is president — Prince Metternich, vice president.

In the same manner the judicial department is arranged. Every

---

[4] Bohemia is divided into sixteen circles.

domain has a *justiziar*, a lawyer by profession, who is equally subject to the proprietor of the domains, as far as he is salaried by him. He decides in the first instance, and is assisted by a secretary and several inferior clerks: the litigant parties, if not content with the sentence of the *justiziar*, may resort to the second tribunal, the Court of Appeal, which holds its sittings in the capital of the kingdom, and is composed of a president, a vice president, and twenty-five counselors. If the Court of Appeal confirms the sentence of the first instance, no farther appeal is possible: if not, the parties may forward their cause to the Supreme Aulic Tribunal of Justice at Vienna, headed by the Minister of Justice. The Government has taken care to protect the peasants from the oppression of the lords and their directors; and the captains of the circles or districts, to whom the domains of the lord, as well as the lands of the peasant, are subject, are a sufficient check on the nobility, if they should attempt to encroach on their subjects through their directors. Still, as the number of masters in authority is infinite, and as the poor peasant is subject to all of them, his share of personal freedom, as obtained by Joseph II, is little better than real slavery.

The character of these peasants is such as one might expect from a people depressed by a crowd of masters, everyone of whom thinks himself entitled to make them sensible of his superiority. They are slavish, insidious, treacherous! There is a gloom brooding on the countenance of the Bohemian, or, as he prefers to style himself, Czech, which makes him unfeeling and stubbornly indifferent to your money or your offers; and he rejects every argument except that *ad hominem*. Music is the only thing which clears up his melancholy brow. It is astonishing what a deep sense the Bohemian of the lowest class has of music. The gloomy stare of his countenance brightens; his sharp gray eyes kindle and beam with fire and sensibility; the whole man is changed. Nothing can exceed the dignity and harmony of the sacred music. When at Raudnitz, we entered a village church, attracted by the long-drawn cadences and the solemn concords of an organ, joined by the voices of the whole congregation. The melancholy air of the music, the sadness so visibly expressed in the countenances of the singers, gave to the whole an interesting character, which it would be difficult to describe.

The Slav nations,(N-5) Russians, Poles, and Bohemians, are

celebrated for their musical talents, especially the *mall* tunes, and their romantic turn. There is hardly any people more inclined to the marvelous, and more fond of tales, than the Bohemians. Without being very superstitious, they dwell with rapture on the deeds of their ancestors. They know by tradition the history of their first dukes — Czech Krock, of his three daughters, and of the founder of their dynasty, Premysl. They will show the traveler, on his passage from Teplitz to Prague, near Welwarn, a solitary barren mountain, where one of their first dukes and warriors with 500 of his followers lies asleep, waiting for the thunderclap which is to rouse him and lay open the doors of his prison, from whence he will sally forth to deliver his countrymen from the yoke of the foreigners, whom they call *hiemezy*, intruders. They have their Amazons, and will show you near Prague the ruins of a castle, once the seat of these heroines: but what excites more than anything else their enthusiasm, is their King Charles IV, son of John, who fell in the battle of Crécy. There will scarcely be found a peasant who knows not exactly the sayings and doings of this excellent prince, while one would ask two millions-and-a-half of them in vain who was the father of the present emperor! This is the more extraordinary as the Austrian monarchs, since the revolution in 1618, did everything in their power to extirpate the national spirit of this people. The public and literary records, and they were certainly far from being indifferent, when we consider the time in which they originated, were not only destroyed by literary *auto da fes* of the Jesuits,(N-6) but every attempt to write an unprejudiced national history was punished in a manner which discouraged even the boldest to sacrifice his existence, and to linger away his life in an Austrian dungeon. Even a member of the princely family of Lobkowitz, Bohuslaus, fell a victim to his desire to enlighten his countrymen! He died in a dungeon. They have, as well as other Catholic countries, their share of superstition, and thousands of coarse statues and paintings decorate their houses, streets, roads, and paths; but the Virgin Mary excepted, these saints are all their own countrymen; they would not even look at a foreign saint. I expressed my astonishment at the thousands who flocked to the shrine of St. John de Nepomuk at Prague: it is, I was told, the only record of our national existence which is left to us, and we celebrate with his fête at once that of our ancient and glorious kings, in whose times he lived. They feel deeply that they are oppressed; they feel it, still more, at the present period. The Bohemian is rather fanatic than religious or superstitious: their priests have less influence than in other Catholic countries of equal intellectual standing, though, before Joseph II, this country teemed with monasteries and monks of every description, introduced by Ferdinand II, to subdue them the more effectually. The suspicious temper of the Bohemian makes him behold, in these priests, the instruments of Government; and though the followers of Huss and Hieronymus of Prague have been extirpated with fire and sword, and are even now, if detected, rewarded with fifty lashes on their posteriors, yet they are still very numerous, under the cloak of Lutheranism.

CHAPTER III

Prague. – Sitting of the Diet of Bohemia. – Nobility of Bohemia. – Private Theater of Count Clam-Gallas. – Musical Conservatorium. – Technical Institution. – Museum. – University. – The System of Education in the Austrian Empire–its consequence. – Secret Police.

THE view of Prague, from the road of Teplitz, is imposing; you descend into a valley extending for five miles, and amphitheatrically rising towards the west: it terminates in a ridge, which runs obliquely the breadth of the whole city. On this ridge stands the Imperial castle, an immense front of colossal buildings, seen at the distance of ten miles. You pass through an indifferent suburb, a half-ruined gate, and enter a street scented by numerous kitchens in the front of the houses. It terminates in a Gothic tower, which separates the city from the new town, Neustadt, laid out by Charles IV. Before this tower two streets diverge, from 150 to 200 feet wide. This part of the town is by far the most regular; it consists almost entirely of noblemen's palaces, and some excellent hotels, among which the Schwarze Ross (black horse) holds the first rank. You thence pass, in the company of your cicerone, a hanger-on at the said hotel, (and, by-the-by, your spy), through the gate of the before-mentioned tower, a relic of Charles IV, and a street whose buildings bespeak the sixteenth, and its irregular dimensions the twelfth century: it runs out into the great marketplace of the ancient city. The city house, a venerable-looking building of the thirteenth century, before whose portal many a noble head has fallen a victim to ill-planned revolutions against the House of Austria; the stately and ancient architecture of the houses in general, and especially the Gothic Church of the Tyn, deserve attention. It has two steeples, 200 feet high, one of which, however, lost its turreted slate roof by a stroke of lightning, and has been replaced by a very poor shingle roof, to guard this noble monument of Gothic architecture on each side. The lower part of the church itself is entirely hidden by a row of houses through which you enter the church: its interior exhibits a striking resemblance to the cathedral of Nôtre Dame in Paris. Among the monuments, that of Tycho Brahe is conspicuous. Through a labyrinth of crooked, narrow streets, which show rather too plainly, that the founder of this renowned city, the Duke Premysl, was anything but a mathematician, you come to the mansion of Count Clam-Gallas, the noblest palace in Prague. It was built by one of his ancestors, after a plan drawn by Michelangelo, and consists of a center and two wings. The two main entrances are guarded by four caryatids, on which the balconies rest. The parapets are decorated with statues of a workmanship rather above mediocrity. Architecture, sculpture, everything combines to make it one of the most superb palaces of the nobility. A street more irregular, if possible, than the former, runs along the ci-devant college of the Jesuits, which contains not less than two large churches and five chapels. Through the gate of a second beautiful tower, from which the students of Prague resisted successfully the invading Swedes in 1648, you enter the bridge, which is disfigured by twenty-eight stands of coarsely executed statues. A third gate receives you, which unites two Gothic towers, which protect the bridge from this side. The small town commences here, built on an ascent which leads across the main place, divided into two parts by a second college of the Jesuits, little inferior to the former in size. It is the seat of the Tribunal of Appeal, of the Court of Justice for the nobility, and of several other offices. A range of magnificent palaces issues from this square; and a turn to your right, places you before the Imperial castle. It consists of two colossal wings connected by a center. The southern wing runs along the before-mentioned ridge, and forms a straight line, at least a thousand yards long, with the chapter of the Nobles Dames, and the palace of Prince Lobkowitz: The chief front looks toward the west. Three gates open to it, decorated with the emblems of Austria and Bohemia. From the open hall in the center, two flights of stairs lead to the Imperial apartments. We passed a noble staircase, the first, second, and third guardroom, and entered the audience chamber. The rooms are lofty, painted, and hung with Flemish pictures; but with the exception of a huge couch of state, with a corresponding tester, cushions, and mattresses, of red damask, there is not the least furniture. Through a corridor, on the left side of which is the Imperial chapel, we passed to the Bohemian salon (Böhmischen Saal), where the Diet of the kingdom was then sitting: it was on the 15th of

August. The avenues to the Imperial castle, the courtyards, and the staircase which leads into the sitting chamber, were lined with the national guards. The salon is a square chamber with two entrances. Opposite the one through which the members of the Diet enter, a platform is raised, on which a chair is placed, the whole surmounted by a canopy, which was elevated; the Supreme Burggrave, as President of the Diet, being only a count by birth: had he been a prince, it would have been lowered. When the Imperial Commissaries entered, the whole assembly rose. The Supreme Burggrave, standing under the canopy, descended the three steps, and complimented them; after which the members of the Diet took their seats. To the right hand sat the Archbishop, as Primate of the kingdom, covered with his pallium, and decorated with the insignia of an Imperial order; next to him, three bishops in their purple robes; the abbots, in black or white silk gowns, with gold chains and crosses. The benches in front of the canopy were occupied by the lords of the kingdom; the second order dressed in their national costume — a red coat, richly embroidered with silver, epaulettes of the same, white breeches, silk stockings, and a three-cornered hat with bullions. Many of them bore orders; almost all the insignia of an Imperial chamberlain — a golden key. The knights occupied the benches on the left, and were dressed in the same manner. The representatives of the cities were in black. The Supreme Burggrave addressed at first the Prince Archbishop and the spiritual lords, in the Bohemian language; then the temporal lords of the kingdom, princes, counts, and barons; afterwards the knights (Ritterstand); and last, the representatives of the cities. Then, complimentary addresses being over, one of the secretaries read the Imperial proposition respecting the taxes to be laid upon the kingdom for the ensuing year. They were received in silence with a low bow. The Supreme Burggrave asked finally, whether any of the members had to propose matters respecting the good of the kingdom. A deep silence reigned throughout the splendid assembly: at last, the Burggrave thanked them in the name of their august sovereign for their ready attendance, and the assembly broke up.

This pageant is the remains of the constitution which Bohemia enjoyed for more than 300 years: its form is still the same, but the spirit is gone. Regularly there are two Diets held every year: Postulate and Extraordinary Diets. For both, the Imperial invitation is issued to the different members, viz. the prelates of the kingdom as the first order, composed of the Archbishop of Prague, the Bishops of Leitmeritz, Königgrätz, Budweis, with several abbots. The second are the lords possessed of domains whose number may amount to a hundred. The knights possessed of domains constitute the third class. The fourth are the four cities, Prague, Budweis, Pilsen, and Königgrätz, whose citizens have the right to buy or possess domains, and the privilege of being represented by their burgomasters and aldermen. Two commissaries from among the lords and knights, are chosen by the Emperor to represent him. They are brought in the state carriage and six of the Supreme Burggrave to the sitting chamber. The real power of the states is now limited to the repartition of the taxes, and a certain jurisdiction which they still exercise through a committee of eight members chosen from among the four orders, and confirmed by the Emperor. The Austrian monarchs thought it necessary to spare the feelings of a nobility and a nation, which cling with cherishing fondness to their ancient liberty, or rather national existence: for, it is but fair to state, that the condition of the peasantry has been improved, especially since the times of Joseph. The real constitutional liberty before rested entirely in the hands of the nobility, of whose power we may form an idea from the strange privileges which they enjoyed, and one of which was, that every lord was entitled to the virginity of his domain; every new-married peasant having been obliged to carry his bride at a certain hour before the door of his lord, and to fetch her home again the next morning. But even for these improvements of their condition, the Bohemian peasant is but little obliged to the sovereigns, who deprived him of his national existence. The difference between the Bohemians and Germans, in this respect, is striking. While the latter, a few attorneys and politicians excepted, will scarcely take any interest in their assemblies, and consider them, what they in their present state really are, rather a nuisance, the former will ask, with a curiosity bordering on anguish, "What has been decided in the Diet?" and turn pale and downcast when they hear of nothing but taxes.

What a powerful thing national feeling is, we may learn by the contrast existing between the Bohemians, Poles, and even Hungarians. Their looks speak. Their mournful countenances, when they hear the name of a free country pronounced; their clenching of the teeth when they hear of Great Britain's free sons; and their inexpressible sadness when their own country is mentioned, the battles they had to fight for a strange cause, the armies they have to recruit and to pay, for their own oppression, and for the scepter of a family who are strangers to them and their interest, though for centuries their masters — and who, in their imbecility, see only the means of keeping them in subjection, and crippling their national resources. An intuitive national feeling and hatred towards foreigners, especially Germans, are among the characteristic features of the Slav nations.

The Poles, under the Austrian dominion, will readily acknowledge that their condition is far better than that of their countrymen who are under the sway of Russia. But the idea of being governed by foreigners and strangers, is alone sufficient to drive them mad; and they rose up in arms against Austria during the disastrous war of 1809, choosing rather to submit to the still more tyrannical scepter of Russia, their brother nation, than to Austria. After the session was over, we visited the Bohemian Chamber; the same where, in the year 1618, the Imperial commissaries, Count Slawata and Martinitz, were thrown out of the windows, by the adherents of Frederick the Palatine. This summary manner of showing their patriotism failed, however, of the expected success, and the Imperial commissaries in a fall of nearly eighty yards, escaped without breaking their necks, through the intervention of a dung hill.

From the third courtyard, we entered the Cathedral of St. Vitus, situated in the center of the Imperial castle, with its appendages the chapter of the Noble Dames and the palace of the Prince Lobkowitz. Its size is moderate, but its decorations are so beautiful, its pointed columns and arches so noble, and its sculptured beauties so superior to those of other Gothic monuments, that one cannot help forming a high idea of the state of Bohemia, when under its own kings. It is not the most beautiful, but certainly the prettiest Gothic church on the continent; begun and finished under Charles IV. His tomb is close to the main entrance. Two marble figures, representing him and his Imperial consort, are stretched upon the mausoleum, their hands crossed, their heads crowned, at their feet the emblem of the kingdom, an erect lion with a double tail. Farther up are the monuments of the Emperors Matthias and Rudolf, the last kings of Bohemia who resided in Prague. In the right aisle is the shrine of one of the patrons of the kingdom, St. John de Nepomuk, confessor to the consort of Wenceslas, the cruel son of Charles IV. This monarch, in a fit of drunkenness and jealousy, caused John to be thrown from the bridge into the Moldau, because he pertinaciously refused to reveal the confession of the queen. Of course he was canonized, and his tongue is there shown to the pious believer, fresh and well preserved, for more than 300 years. The quantity of silver and gold on his shrine amounts to £4000. When the rumor of its being doomed to the same fate as the rest of the treasures of the churches, spread over the country, thousands of Bohemians left their homes to bid farewell to their national property. The gloomy and menacing silence of the pilgrims saved this treasure. The Government thought it prudent to spare the feelings of an oppressed people, and the order was revoked. On the same side is the Imperial lodge, and the chapel of St. Wenceslas, the first Christian duke who paid for his piety with his life. He was murdered by his brother, Boleslaus, at the instigation of his mother, Drohomira.

The square, which extends in front of the Imperial castle, is lined with several palaces, among which those of the Duke of Reichstadt and of the Archbishop, are conspicuous; the former was the residence of the Emperor Alexander, and the latter of the King of Prussia, during the Congress at Prague.

The view from the terrace of the castle over the whole extensive city, with its numberless churches, towers, and palaces, its bridge stained with the hue of age, the wide river with its beautiful islands and parks, is a noble sight. It is the true picture of a once powerful hierarchy, and still wealthy nobility, struggling with the impending decay of their own power and of their country. There are about forty ancient Bohemian families, who may be said to constitute the leading aristocracy of the kingdom: their estates amount to nearly two-thirds of the landed property, including their peasants. The most distinguished among them are the families of the Princes Lobkowitz, Schwarzenberg, Kinsky; the Counts Harrach, Clam-Martinez, Schlick, Chotek, Wrbna, Wrtby, Kolowrat, Czernin, Waldstein, Sternberg, and Nostiz. These are considered as Bohemian families; whereas the Princes Liechtenstein, Dietrichstein, Colloredo-Mansfeld, Auersperg,

Windischgrätz, Clary, Kaunitz, Salm, Thun, are reckoned among the German families, though they are possessed of large estates in the kingdom. Most of their possessions are donations of the Austrian Emperor, who, by these amalgamating means, desired to break the spirit of the national nobility, and succeeded in his wishes. The former took an active part in the fatal war of 1809. They raised battalions from among their subjects, and many also equipped them and put themselves at their head. The great sums which they were to take up, the subsequent wars of 1813 and of 1814, the increasing taxes even after these wars, the natural consequences of a bad financial management of an expensive prime minister, a secret policy and high standing in the political sphere, contributed not a little to damp their spirits.

Bohemia is, without doubt, the most oppressed and least favored of all the provinces and kingdoms of the Austrian Empire. Though Bohemia, with its appendage, Moravia, has not more than five millions of inhabitants, the sixth part of the population of the Austrian Empire, yet these two provinces bear not less than a third of the whole expenses and contributions, and furnish more troops than the kingdom of Hungary with ten millions of inhabitants. What adds to the mortification of this people, is the indifference shown to their interest. Its principal river, the Elbe, flowing through the finest part of the kingdom, it was thought proper to insure to the inhabitants the export of their produce to Hamburg. The treaty of navigation, as concluded by the Austrian envoy, the favorite of Metternich, now president of the German Diet at Frankfurt, bears evident marks of being dictated by a policy which is afraid of seeing this people in contact with the Germans. Of course, Metternich and the present system is not looked upon in the most favorable light by the national nobility, and they are in silent opposition to his measures.

We visited, the day after our arrival, the private theater of Count Clam-Gallas, a nobleman who, for his patriotic feeling and his incessant exertions to counterpoise the dead weight of despotism, deserves universal praise. The night's performance was Schiller's Maria Stuart. I was particularly struck with the part acted by the Countess Schlick, as Queen Elizabeth; and Mrs. Siddons herself would have acknowledged her *dilettante* rival an incomparable representative of this proud and selfish prude, yet still great character.

This, however, was but a faint prelude to Goethe's Torquato Tasso, performed a week later, the inimitable picture of high life. It is almost impossible to draw the line of demarcation closer, to paint the delicate *nuances* of a love checked by courtly haughtiness and sneering contempt, which the prince of German poets draws so masterly in Tasso, far better than Prince Thurn and Taxis, and Count Thun. They moved in their own sphere, and their play was natural. It looks strange to see noblemen and ladies on the boards, and in the *cothurnus*; but they are forced into this monopoly. Though the public theater was built at their own expense and supported in a way suitable to the resources of a moderate kingdom, yet the Emperor, afraid lest his subjects should grow wanton from the intellectual enjoyments of classic or liberal works, ordered not only their mutilation, but most of Schiller's works, which are even performed on the Vienna stage, to be here entirely prohibited; they are less trusted than the Austrians. The nobility themselves perform in this private theater, and none but noblemen of their rank, or strangers who are introduced into their circles, are admitted.

The public opera is still above mediocrity, its orchestra unrivaled. The Bohemians have a singularly fine ear for instrumental music, and perform *con amore*. When Mozart had composed his *chef-d'œuvre*, Don Giovanni, he hastened to Prague to lay his work before a public, which, as he expressed himself, was alone capable of giving a correct opinion of the merits of his production. It was accordingly performed through three successive nights. The enthusiasm increased with every performance. When he returned to Vienna, this masterpiece met there with a cold reception; the Emperor Joseph was present during the performance. Mozart was called before the monarch: — "Mozart," said the monarch, "your music would do very well, but there are too many notes in it!" — "Just as many," replied the offended artist, "as there ought to be!"(N-7)

The Bohemian nobility have, with a proper sense of the musical bias of their countrymen, established an institution, which furnishes not only first-rate *virtuosos* for their own chapels, but for which Europe in general ought to be grateful. Sixty pupils, twenty of whom are females, are instructed in the different branches of instrumental and vocal music by twelve teachers, who are salaried by the nobility. Of the great musical talents which have been fostered in this conservatorium, we name only Madame Sonntag.

The Technical Academy, equally called into existence by the nobility, and supported entirely by them, was our next visit: its director is the Chevalier Gerstner, a gentleman whose mathematical eminence is respected throughout Europe. The furnaces of Genitz, and Horshowitz, and Purglitz, the road to Carlsbad, and several other buildings, are his works.(N-8) He has under him four professors. The number of pupils amounts to 150. They are here taught mathematics in all its branches. The Museum of Prague is an interesting collection of Bohemian and Slav antiquity. Besides manuscripts, works of sculpture and of the pencil, there are offensive and defensive weapons, bucklers, swords of an immense size, one of the shoes of Premysl, the first Duke of Bohemia, the fauna of this country, with a number of other curiosities. The salon, where the works of the ancient Bohemian literature are deposited, is the most interesting. They had in the fourteenth century their historians, civilians, lawyers, divines, and poets, of whom we know little or nothing, and who might spread over this dark age a light of which we never dreamed. But they are chained down: their publication is prohibited, and as they are mostly writers in the Bohemian language, they may be considered as dead treasures. Among the Bohemian painters, Raphael, Mengs, Skreta, and Brandel, rank high. A Salvator and a Joseph by Skreta, are particularly remarkable for their coloring and truth of expression. There is a Saviour by Brandel painted with the finger. Seen closely, this picture presents a chaos of colors laid on finger-thick, not unlike the daubing of a child. From a distance of six yards, however, it melts into one of the divinest and noblest ideals of Our Lord. The liberality with which the nobility founded this monument of national arts and sciences, and contributed towards it from their own galleries, armories, and libraries, shows plainly that national feeling and honor are far from being extinct. They collected with great expense, since the foundation of this museum in 1818, the remains of past grandeur from the remotest corners of Europe, from Sweden and Russia; and though they are not yet allowed to make any use of them, still they seem to look forward to a more favorable period.

Of the 30,000 students who are said to have crowded, in the times of Charles IV and his successors, the salons of the renowned university at Prague, but 1000 remain.(N-9) These are trained according to the pleasure of his Imperial Majesty, as expressed when the professors were admitted into his Imperial presence, in 1825. "I will have my subjects learn all those things that are useful in common life, and likely to keep them attached to our person and to their religion. I don't want teachers who fill the heads of my students with that nonsense which turns the brains of so many youths in our days." The only scientific branch allowed a free range is medicine. The others, in 1822, received a warning which will cut off all redundant study during the Emperor's life. Of the members of this university, the Professor of Philosophy Bolzano was universally admitted to be one of the very first. Several works which he published, showed him to be a very liberal and eminent thinker. This gentleman was suddenly arrested, his writings seized, himself placed before an ecclesiastical tribunal, at the head of which was the archbishop, to answer the charge of heterodoxy. The poor archbishop, a good, kind-hearted, simple old man, universally beloved, was, one may suppose, not a little puzzled to manage this dogmatical trial, out of whose labyrinth of nonsense the Pope, with all his infallibility, would not have extricated himself: he succeeded, however, in clearing the doctor of the crime of heterodoxy; but all his endeavors, together with those of the nobility, to obtain his re-admission to the philosophical chair were unsuccessful. "Let me alone," said the Emperor, when the P———ss L———y interceded on his behalf. "He has dangerous, extravagant principles." One of his disciples, a director of the theological seminary in Leitmeritz, went a step farther, and asserted, as was said, in one of his lectures, that those doctrines, which are incompatible with human reason, cannot be founded on divine precepts. This daring speech resounded in Vienna, and a few weeks afterwards the confessor of his Majesty, Mr. Frint, arrived with two commissaries from Vienna, arrested the poor director, and carried him under escort to Vienna, where he was imprisoned with the Liguorians. The bishop, under whose eyes this *ne plus ultra* of infidelity took place, was deprived of his see, and sent into a Capuchin monastery. These three examples have proved effectual in curing the spirit of the Bohemian literati, and they are now plodding on according to the manner prescribed.

As the system of studies, as it is called, is throughout the Austrian Empire the same, it may not be superfluous to give a succinct idea of it. There are, besides the university, three lyceums or colleges, and twenty-five gymnasiums or Latin schools in Bohemia. The university has, besides, a rector magnificus, whose office however is a mere title, and who is chosen annually with four directors, two of which, the directors of philosophy and of divinity, are clergymen. The director of the gymnasiums and of the lyceums, is also a priest. They are under the control of a counselor of the Government, to whom they make their reports. The elementary schools are equally under the supreme direction of a clergyman, who is in the same manner answerable to the Government.(N-10) Private teaching is not allowed. The youth, after having run through the elementary schools, passes into the Latin schools or gymnasiums; in which he is instructed for the ensuing four years, in the Latin language and in religion; the two following years he reads extracts from Latin authors, and the elements of the Greek language; two hours in the week are allotted to religion, mathematics, geography, and history. Each gymnasium has one prefect, six professors, and a teacher of religion. In six years the youth has completed his gymnasial studies, and is advanced to the university. There he hears, for the first year, extracts of philosophy, religion, history, mathematics, the elements of the Greek language; again, in the second year, the same, with the exception of mathematics, for which physic and astronomy are substituted. In the third year, he reads the history of the German Empire, and aesthetics. The students are not allowed to choose for themselves; the professors or lecturers are all obliged to pursue the same course. These three years being passed, the youth chooses either law, divinity, or medicine. In the former two courses, he continues his studies four, in the latter five years. The whole course of studies takes thus thirteen, and in medicine, fourteen years. The schoolbooks for all these different classes, except medicine, are compiled in Vienna, under the superintendence of the Aulic Commission of Studies. They are subject to such alterations as a newly-created counselor of the court thinks fit to suggest, according to his own or his Emperor's notions. These schoolbooks are the most barren and stupid extracts which ever left the printing press. The professors are bound, under penalty of losing their places, to adhere literally to these skeletons.

At Easter, and towards the close of August, the youth is examined: if his answers prove satisfactory, he is admitted at the beginning of the next year into a higher class; if otherwise, he is detained till he knows by heart his lesson, and then advanced. A young man who has gone through the academic course of these studies, knows a little of everything, but on the whole nothing. He has regularly forgotten in the succeeding course, what he had learned by heart in the preceding. A free exercise of the mental powers, a literary range is absolutely impossible; nay, against the instructions of the professors. The youth, during the time of his studies, is watched with the closest attention. His professors are ex-officio spies. Six times in the year he has to confess himself to his teachers of religion! — His predilections, inclinations, his good and bad qualities, every movement is observed and registered in their catalogues; one of which is sent to Vienna, the other to the Government, the third deposited in the school archives. This observation increases as the youth advances into the higher classes, and a strict vigilance is paid to his reading; trials are made with classic authors, his opinion is elicited about characters such as Brutus, Cato, and the account thereof faithfully inserted. If the youth applies to law, the scrutiny becomes still more vigorous, and his principles about the natural rights of man and of Government are extorted under a thousand shapes and pretenses.

The youth, having finished his academic course, whether he be a lawyer, or a divine, is entirely in the hands of the Government. His past life and conduct serve his superiors as a guide. Has he given the least cause of suspicion, shown the least *penchant* towards liberal ideas? then he may be sure that the higher his talents, the less his capacity to serve his Emperor, or to obtain a license as an attorney. Should he apply to the Government for a non-commissioned office, his immediate superiors become again his watchmen. An unguarded word is sufficient not only to preclude his advancement, but to deprive him even of his station. He cannot expect indulgence or forbearance on the part of his superiors; it would be looked upon as a connivance, and if repeated, deprive them of their places.

There are, in every department among the counselors or assessors, at least two spies, who correspond regularly with the President of the Supreme Police at Vienna, or with the Emperor himself. Two months before my arrival, the most distinguished counselor of the Government expressed his opinion, in the sittings of this tribunal, which is headed by the chief of the kingdom, the Supreme Burggrave, respecting a question about duties on imported produce. He availed himself of this opportunity to give a comprehensive and clear statement of the system in all its bearings, saying, that the present system was not in accordance with the state of manufactures. He was speaking this at the same time that his preferment to the Supreme Financial Department, as Aulic Counselor, wanted only the signature of the Emperor, after having been recommended by the financial department, and approved by the State Council. What was the astonishment of this counselor, when, eight days afterwards, the appointment of the youngest counselor of the Government arrived from Vienna, signed by the Emperor, who wrote with his own hand that a man who looked more at the spirit of the time, than at the expressed will of his monarch, could not be a fit subject for a counselor of the court, and that his Majesty did not want reasoners, but faithful servants. There is no Aulic counselor of the Department of Justice who would dare to ask his colleague of the financial branch respecting the measures of his department; it would be looked upon as a temptation or as an interference with objects in which he has not, and should not take any concern, though it may be that, in a fortnight, he is appointed to the very committee or department, of the measures of which, to inform himself beforehand, would be considered as presumptuous and dangerous. When Count O'Donnel, Minister of Finances, died, the Emperor, then at Prague, looked round for a successor, and the then-Supreme Burggrave, Count Wallis, was called before him. "Count," he was accosted, "I am going to reward you for your faithful services. O'Donnel is dead, I have designated you for his successor."—"Your Majesty," replied the Count, "will most graciously condescend to consider that I am entirely ignorant in this department, as I have never paid the least attention to it."—"That is what I want; never mind, you will learn it," resumed the Emperor; "everyone to his business. You were a faithful Supreme Burggrave, you will be a no-less faithful Finance Minister." The consequence was, as might be expected, a bankruptcy, which, in the financial history, will be recorded as disgraceful as the battle of Ulm, which was owing to nearly the same cause. These explanations will fully account for the painful ignorance, servility, and narrowness of conception of the Austrian officers, both civil and military. Out of a thousand secretaries, counselors, and assessors, who have run through the whole course of studies, you will not find fifty who can give you an explanation of the financial state of the Empire. Out of a thousand Austrian captains, there will not be fifty who have the least idea of tactics, except those of the artillery and engineers. These gentlemen advance colonels, generals, field marshals, lieutenants, not by dint of military prowess or knowledge, but according to the rule of seniority; while the others, plodding on in the same way, become counselors of the court, of the state, and the managers of the household of the Emperor. Thus, while we see poor countries like Saxony and Prussia prospering, paying off their debts, and establishing a firm national credit; their armies, with a soldiery far inferior to the Austrian in discipline and military prowess, fighting their battles successfully: the Austrian Empire with its immense resources, is impoverished, every day more and more, through the ignorance of their financial men; and, owing to the same cause, their armies are beaten and captured like so many herds of cattle, through the supine idiotism of their commanders.

There are several omens which have induced his Imperial Majesty to direct his attention not only to his officers, whom he considers less as public servants than as his own, but to the inhabitants generally. In a country where the lower classes are servile and ignorant, the feeling of honor, of course, very precarious, it requires little pains for the agents of the police to induce servants to betray their masters. For every information the former carry to the police, they obtain one or two ducats. During my stay, a merchant gave a dinner to several of his friends. The conversation turned on the new loan. Everyone gave his opinion, which was unfavorable to the measure. Next day he was called before the Chief of the Police, to account for the language used at his party. The merchant pleaded his right to discuss public pecuniary affairs: but he was answered, that it was no business of his, as he was not a banker; and that a repetition of such disrespectful language would be punished with imprisonment!

The merchant returned home and instantly dismissed his servants, being convinced of their having betrayed him. He is again summoned to answer the cause of the dismissal of his servants. Again he pleads his right to do as he pleases; and the Director and Chief of the Police, an Imperial Counselor of the Government, holding the rank of a colonel, and a Knight of an Order, has the impudence to assure him upon his honor, that he did not get his information from the servants! It is impossible to form an adequate idea of the ramifications of this product of a bad public conscience. Every footman in a public house is a salaried spy: there are spies paid to visit the taverns and hotels, who take their dinners at the *table d'hôte*. Others will be seen in the Imperial library for the same purpose, or in the bookseller's shop, to inquire into the purchases made by the different persons. Of course, letters sent and received by the poet, if the least suspicious, are opened; and so little pains are taken to conceal this violation of public faith, that the seal of the post office is not seldom added to that of the writer. These odious measures are not executed with that *finesse* which characterizes the French, nor with the military rudeness of the Prussian, but in that silly and despicable way of the Austrian, who, as he is the most awkward personage for this most infamous of all commissions, takes, notwithstanding, a sort of pride in being an Imperial instrument and a person of importance. One characteristic feature of this Government is particularly striking: its persecution turns less against foreigners than the people who communicate with them. They and their families are exposed to every sort of chicanery; and for this reason, it is almost impossible to associate, if we except noblemen, with the better classes, all of them dreading the crafty severity of their suspicious Government.

Without introduction into the circles of the nobility, it would be, indeed, impossible for a man of even the most moderate pretensions to stay in this city for a week, every enjoyment being poisoned by the baneful influence of the secret police. The middle class of its inhabitants are a sober, well-informed, and respectable set, far above the sensuality of the Viennese; though the Government does not allow even those scanty means of public information which the latter possess. In Prague there is but one, and this the poorest newspaper imaginable, under the immediate control of the Supreme Burggrave. Another public paper in the Bohemian language had hardly made its appearance with the consent of the Government, when it was suppressed by an order from Vienna.

Taken in the whole, Prague is one of the most picturesque and noble cities on the continent; far more interesting than Berlin, or any other capital of Germany. What, however, entitles this city to our attention, are the immense historical treasures which it possesses respecting the origin of their own and of their kindred nations, the Russians and Poles. A universal history, without a peregrination to the shelves of ancient Maroboduus, will certainly be, with respect to the Slav nations, but very imperfect. The line of demarcation which, not withstanding an allegiance of three centuries to the House of Austria, still separates this people from the Austrians, is no way astonishing; and a Hampden, or, to speak in their own language, a Ziska, in the present gloom, would scarcely fail to find at least a million adherents.

CHAPTER IV

Tour from Prague through Moravia and Austria. – The Empire of Great Moravia, Austria. – Vineyards. – Villages. – Inhabitants, their condition. – Church festivities. – Austrian Abbeys. – Hierarchy. – Pliability of the Clergy. – Rudolf of Habsburg and his successors.

THE road from Prague through Moravia and Austria boasts very little interest. A well-cultivated country, a village, or a small town every five or ten miles, with a dirty tavern, and still dirtier bedrooms, and some country residences of noblemen, inferior, however, to those between Prague and Teplitz, are the only cursory objects. Thirty-five miles from Prague, the heights of Kolin present themselves, where Frederick the Great lost a battle and the glory of invincibility. We passed ten miles farther through Czaslau, and about eighty-five miles south from Prague, over the frontiers of Bohemia, marked by a pyramid with a lion carved in relief, facing Bohemia, and an erect eagle turned towards Moravia. Of the powerful empire of Great Moravia, whose kings swayed a territory stretching from the Danube to the Gulf of Finland, the name only remains. The last king of this monarchy, Zwentibold, was vanquished by the German Emperor Arnulf, his monarchy divided, and part of it annexed to Bohemia, under the name of Moravia. The unhappy monarch himself was obliged to exchange his scepter for the staff; and his very residence, Welehrad, was turned into a monastery, of which he became the first abbot. Though Moravia has been separated from Bohemia since its acquisition by Austria, and erected into a distinct Government, yet its manners, language, and dress, all bespeak a people intimately blended with the Bohemians. The state of the peasantry, and of the nobility, is entirely the same with those of Bohemia; there is, as in this kingdom, a Diet enjoying the same form, the same privileges, and equally devoid of substance. The first place which we entered is Iglau, a handsome town, with 10,000 inhabitants, and extensive wool manufactures. The country round Iglau is cold and dreary: forty-five miles south is Znaim, the last point where the

Bohemian language is spoken. There is something tenacious in this people which exceeds belief. The northern suburbs of this town keep still to their Bohemian tongue, as they did three hundred years ago; while in the southern part, I was told that scarcely a person could be found to understand it. In the same proportion the character of the people changes. Not a trace is to be found of the dark gloomy character of the Bohemian, approaching to misanthropy. There is no transition, no blending between the two nations; they are separated like Germans and French, and a union of three hundred years cannot stifle this antipathy, nor bring them to forget the nicknames with which they honor each other.

The distance from Znaim to Vienna is thirty miles on the Imperial road. The more interesting road is, however, through Retz, Krems, and Sankt Pölten. We took the latter. The country from Znaim westward is almost an uninterrupted vineyard, softly rising and descending on the eminences, and now and then interrupted by an orchard or by wheat fields in the lower grounds. There is a calm, a hilarity spread over the whole, which is reflected in the laughing countenances of the lads and maids employed in stripping the vines of their superfluous branches and leaves, to hasten the ripening of the grapes. Many as we met, all of them offered us grapes. As the forerunners of the villages are always the same wine cellars, at the distance of fifty yards. They are dug into the ground, and generally vaulted. The entrance to them is through a stone building, containing the winepress, and a room or two for the entertainment of the proprietor and wine buyers. Wagons loading for Vienna, Bohemia, or Moravia, are waiting before the doors, and, as this trade cannot be carried on without frequent libations, we were sure of being invited at every such stand to share in them. These cellars, from forty to fifty in number, are each overshadowed by walnut trees, which guard the entrance; two benches and a table are commonly raised under them. The villages themselves bespeak a serenity and a wealth which you will not find elsewhere throughout the continent. A brook is a necessary ingredient to an Austrian village; its banks are lined with willows, horse chestnuts, and walnuts. At some distance the houses run down in long rows. A thatched roof is as great a rarity as a tavern. The inhabitants being cultivators of the grape, prefer to take a glass, or rather a flagon, at home. The houses are from one to two stories high, covered with tiles, and provided with green shutters. On both sides, before the house, are small gardens with green or yellow painted railings, through which the passage to the house door is left open. You enter through a wicket which is in the large door. The first room is the visiting room; it is generally painted, and furnished with an elegant stove, two bureaus, half a dozen chairs, and a sofa. In the midst is a large table covered with a Tyrolian carpet, on which two flagons and a number of tumblers are placed. The other rooms are furnished in a less sumptuous, but clean and substantial manner. Round the green stove, and the white shining walls, runs a row of open benches; round the ceiling, large wine glasses are seen hanging, in which the journeymen receive their daily portion of wine. Some pictures of saints, or an engraving of Maria Theresa, Joseph, or Francis, decorate the walls. This latter is indeed their prototype in everything. They consider him exactly in the light of a father, or rather a guardian, whom they may approach at any time, and to whom they submit in everything. Their characters tally so exactly with that of the Emperor, that from this affinity of thinking there cannot but exist the greatest harmony between the Austrian and his Emperor.

We had passed a dozen of these beautiful villages, each vying with one another in elegance and beauty, and were just going to enter the last, which lay on the road to the small but beautiful town of Retz, where we intended to stay; when, as we lagged after our carriage, an elderly farmer plodding behind us for a while, at last took heart to speak and ask us whither we were bound. Being satisfied on the point, he forced us almost to spend a night under his roof. We had hardly entered the house, when the landlady came with two flagons, one filled with wine, the other with water, to drink the welcome. The time till supper was spent, according to the fashion of the country, in drinking and talking.

Our landlord, an honest and wealthy wine cultivator of Retzbach, had a lawsuit against the lord of the domain, respecting a ward to whom the former was guardian. Determined not to have the suit procrastinated, he went forthwith to see the Emperor Francis. He was of course received, and stated his case. "Have you got the cognizance?" demanded the Emperor. —"Yes, I have," replied the farmer. —"Then I will tell you what," resumed the Emperor; "you had better go to the Aulic Counselor S——z, and let him see it." —"But would it not be better," said the frank Austrian, "if your Majesty would command Mr. Schwarzin to do it?" —"No, my child," said the Emperor, "you don't understand; that business must have its way; I cannot do anything beforehand; go, go, and you will hear what he says, and then come and tell me." He went accordingly to the Counselor S——z, who answered, that he could not do anything before matters were brought to him in the regular course of business. Again he returned to the Emperor, who with the same patience exhorted him to wait, and that he would himself take care and expedite it. The farmer then returned home, and in six weeks his lawsuit was decided in his favor.

The Austrian farmer is a kind-hearted, good-humored being, with a great deal of openness and honesty; which latter two qualities, however, are said to have lost their former value, by the state bankruptcies, the examples of bad faith given them by their Emperor, and the secret police. He is more wealthy than his Bohemian or Polish fellow subjects, and is in fact a freeholder, as bondage and menial offices have been redeemed throughout Austria from the noblemen, with the connivance of the Government, by a certain sum of money. Nothing exceeds his hospitality; and whoever comes is not only welcome, but almost killed with kindness. The Germans are noted for their insatiable thirst. In Austria, the number of emptied flagons is astonishing; but notwithstanding a true Austrian farmer, as we often convinced ourselves, will wash down a sort of pigs' meat, with horseradish, with one, or even two flagons, holding two gallons of wine, he is seldom seen drunk. Custom, and the quality of the wine itself, which is of a light sort, similar to the Rhine wine, only rather more acid, explain this. In order to keep themselves in constant appetite, they advance with every flagon they take, from the inferior to the better sorts; as there are thousands who have a stock of more than 1000 hogsheads in their cellars, from the year 1811 down to 1826. They complain sadly of the French, who emptied their cellars from the vintages of 1783 and 1794; and as it is the highest gratification of their pride to show their wealth in this manner, one may easily imagine the quantity of wine consumed during their fêtes. The principal one is the church wake.

Nothing can exceed the jollity and gaiety of a church festivity in

Austria proper. They are kept every year, on two successive Sundays, in every village. The preparations for the fête are made the week preceding it, by the united efforts of the young single men. The largest tree from the next forest is chosen, stripped of its bark, planed, and surmounted with the crown of a fir tree, bearing the emblems of country life; apples, bottles filled with wine, ribbons, and garlands. This tree is raised in the center of a pavilion, or rather a bower, covered with branches, and hung over with festoons of every color. Each farmer invites his friends of the neighboring villages. After grand mass is over, the dinner is served, consisting of at least twenty different dishes. At three o'clock, after the second divine service, the lads make their appearance, dressed very elegantly, and repair in a body to the different farmhouses where the maidens are. These are conducted in procession to the dancing place, the before-mentioned bower. The orchestra consists of an exquisite band of from ten to fifteen musicians, who regularly attend these festivals. Among their instruments are two lyres, but no violin, which give to the music an exquisite air of country life. There is nothing which equals the waltzes of these people. The most prejudiced enemy to this dance cannot help being delighted with the simplicity and true charm which these dancers display in every turn, without having ever been under the modeling hand and snuffling command of a French dancing master. One might look for hours with interest at the hearty delight with which they enjoy this ancient fête. If distinguished persons are present, they are requested to open the ball, a thing which is always complied with. At sunset lamps are lighted, and the dance continues until eleven o'clock. The maidens are again conducted home in the same manner, and each is delivered into the hands of her parents. It was at the castle and domain of G———k, the property of C———t F———s, where we witnessed one of these fêtes. The family of the Count had partaken for half an hour in the popular rejoicing. For this honor the young people brought them a serenade.

 The castle of G———k is situated on one of the romantic cliffs of the Danube, twenty-five miles above the dreaded Lanenstande, commanding on one side the mighty river, and on the other the beautiful valley with its village. The rocky ground between this and the castle is occupied by a park, from whose clumps of oaks and birches you see peeping out rocks overgrown with moss, which invest the scenery with an inexpressible air of romantic beauty. It was in this park, in the midst of precipices and natural grottoes, the youths and musicians performed the serenade. Of the pieces sung and played, there was none more charming than the beautiful Tyrolian air, "Wenn ich morgens früh aufstehe," [when I rise early in the morning] sung by about forty young men, scattered all over the park. The manly voices of the singers, re-echoing from the surrounding cliffs and mountains, the numerous lights, and the grandeur of the scenery, all contributed to make it one of the most delicious enjoyments. It is singular that this people, certainly one of the best and most kind-hearted on the face of the earth, though endowed with a rather strong *penchant* towards that sort of sensuality which delights in eating and drinking, is so generally hated. There are, however, two reasons: one is their blind obedience towards their sovereign, which makes them, as soon as they become connected in any way with the Government, exceed even their instructions, in order to please their sovereign. They are detested neither for their vices nor for the wrongs they have inflicted, but for the awkward and stolid manner in which they execute the orders of their masters. Again, the Austrian has not the least national pride, nor any of the virtues which spring from this feature. This very circumstance, so excellent in keeping together the ties of the different twenty races and nations who compose the Austrian Empire, and making them less sensible of the prerogative which the Austrian enjoys, has on the other hand caused that contempt towards a people which has so few shining qualities. Almost any nation would think it a disgrace to submit to an Austrian whose plain manners and unseasonable familiarity make him an object of scorn, even when victorious in a foreign province.

From St. Pölten, an ancient town, with an episcopal see, the country towards Vienna assumes a grand aspect. Thousands of isolated farms, buried, as it were, under forests of fruit trees, cover the valleys, while the hills are clad with the most luxuriant vines. On the left you have the lordly Danube, with its mountains overgrown with forests; to the right the lofty mountains of Styria. Several abbeys here attract your attention, and give a great idea of the wealth of the Austrian clergy. We visited the most celebrated of them, Kremsmünster and Klosterneuburg. The first is rather an accumulation of palaces, built in the demi-Italian demi-French style.

The abbey is obliged to keep a seminary for the education of the youth; the library, gallery of paintings, and the apartments of the abbot and the Imperial family, are in the first style. The most interesting is Klosterneuburg, about seven miles above Vienna, on the left bank of the Danube, in a most delightful situation. This magnificent abbey consists of the church in the center, and two wings connected with it by galleries. The one is destined for the Imperial family, the other for the abbot. Behind the palace of the abbot is the convent of the monks. The depth of this edifice corresponds exactly with its height; its cellars are three stories deep, the third and last under the Danube. We saw a wagon and six, loaded with barrels, entering and turning in this immense cavity.

The quantity of wine here stored is not less than 20,000 pipes, raised in part from their own vineyards and from tithes; which latter, as the librarian informed us, amounted to 10,000 pipes, a revenue of about £10,000 They are, however, allowed but a small part of this income; and though they have the management of their economical affairs, yet they have to render an annual account to the Government and to refund the surplus of this allowance. This allowance is, for the abbot 2000 florins; for each monk 300. Their number is limited, too, and they are bound either to apply to the instruction of youth, or to pastoral offices, for lifetime. They elect their abbot in the presence of the Imperial Commissaries, who invest him after the election with the ring, the symbol of his temporal power. He is subject, in his spiritual jurisdiction, to the bishop of the diocese; in his temporal affairs to the Government. There are now comparatively but few abbeys in Austria, and these are throughout regulated on the same footing; those whose inhabitants led a more contemplative life having been abolished by the Emperor Joseph, and their estates added to the religious fund, from which the curates and the secular clergy are salaried. The bishops are nominated by the Emperor, without whose permission no bull of the Pope can be published. They are not only subject to the provincial Governments, but even to the captains of the districts in whose territories their dioceses are situated. The divine service in extraordinary cases is regulated by the Government, as *Te Deums*, processions, etc. The permission of the Captain of the Circle, and if in the capital, that of the Governor, is required. The education of the theologicians, although in the hands of the bishops, is controlled by

Imperial Commissaries. The clergy of the Austrian Empire is thus really stripped of any injurious power, more effectually than in any other country. Compared to the authority which the Emperor of Austria exercises over his archbishops, bishops, and the whole train of these dignitaries, the rights of the Gallican church and of the King of France are only trifles. The means by which the reforms of the Emperor Joseph were carried on consisted merely in a title.

The Emperors of Austria, in their capacity as Kings of Hungary, are born legates of the Roman See. Of the privileges annexed to this dignity, they availed themselves so effectually, that the counselor of the state for the religious department in Austria, M. Lorenz, has indeed more power than the archbishops and bishops,[5] with the Pope of Rome altogether. The hierarchical management of Austria and its canonical laws deserve serious attention and deep study on the part of every statesman. The manner in which the power of the clergy is controlled deserves the highest praise.

As an instance of condescension in the Roman Nuncio, in a country where, notwithstanding a seeming compliance with its head, his Holiness the Pope exercises no authority at all, I may mention the recent conversion of Baron Kleyle, Counselor to the Court. A matrimonial affair brought him over to the Catholic faith. As he was a character of distinction, and rather of a philosophical and skeptical turn of mind, his apostasy from Protestantism was looked upon by the Catholic clergy as a triumph, and the Roman Nuncio condescended so far as to sign certain exceptions, which the Baron made before he entered the bosom of the Catholic Church. The first was, Baron Kleyle could not invoke the saints — left to his own discretion. **II.** His belief in purgatory — he might do as he pleased. **III.** Baron Kleyle could not hear every day a mass — he would not have an objection to hear one on a Sunday. **IV.** He could not confess himself: at least he would please, if possible, to do it once a year. The agreement was signed; the Baron went over, and married his bride.

We approached now, on the road from Klosterneuburg, the famous residence of the Austrian dynasty, alternately the headquarters of Roman legions, of German Margraves, and of an Imperial court.

---

[5] See Rechberger.

Vienna, with its ramparts, which seem to guard the city, and its vast suburbs which surround it at the distance of six hundred yards, is not unlike the Austrian Empire, whose vast kingdom and provinces surround the small archdukedom of Austria proper. Its very palaces, its intricate mazes, and its crooked, narrow, and winding streets, bear the character of tameness, and of that shifting policy for which the reigning family is so justly notorious, far more than that of the different nations whose head this capital has become. This Imperial family is a true specimen how often the greatest events are the offspring of small accidental causes. A count of Switzerland meets, during one of his sporting excursions, a poor priest on his way to administer the sacrament to a dying parishioner. His progress is arrested by a brook, just at the moment when the count with his retinue arrives. Respectfully he offers his own horse to the priest, humbly it is accepted, and the next day returned. "God forbid!" exclaims the count to the messenger, "I should ride a horse again which carried my savior: I bestow it on the church and the priest." This poor priest becomes the chaplain and the confidant of the Prince Elector of Mainz, and his influence prevails on the first spiritual prince of Germany, to propose the pious horse lender to the assembled Electors of this empire. As his military prowess promised to be useful at a time when Germany was infested by numberless petty waylaying knights, and his want of power gave no reason for jealousy, he was accepted, and thus Rudolf, Count of Habsburg, became the first though least powerful monarch of Christendom.

Though a wealthy Count, he was a poor prince; he had, however, a treasure in his daughters, which he disposed of in that prudent way which enabled him with the assistance of his princely sons in law, to deprive Ottocar, the King of Bohemia, of Austria. This dukedom had been seized, after the decease of the last duke of the house of Babenberg, by Ottocar, and was in vain re-demanded by Rudolf. Ottocar was twice defeated; and his death on the field of battle secured the family of Habsburg in that first possession, the Archdukedom of Austria. His successors pursued the same prudent and marrying way, and acquired by these means the kingdoms of Bohemia, Hungary, a number of smaller provinces, and finally the vast Spanish monarchy, till Charles V, the most powerful monarch of Europe, dared to aspire, three hundred years afterwards, to universal monarchy. Without a distinguished character, without even the love of those nations, and in spite of continual revolts, this family not only extricated itself from imminent dangers, but rose from its frequent downfalls more powerful than before. While we see the foundations of other empires shaken where sovereign and people are intimately blended, and liberal ideas are spreading every day, there is in this vast monarchy, till the present time, scarcely a movement perceptible towards emancipation, which none of the nations under this Government seem to require. Where the greatest genius would have failed, the monarchs of Austria have succeeded by the very want of genius; and by merely resorting to such common means as lie nearer to the level of common understandings, are neither visionary nor fantastic, and therefore seldom fail in their intended success.

CHAPTER V

View of Vienna. – Suburbs. – Glacis. – Imperial Castle. – Imperial Apartments. – Guards. – The Emperor.

THE approach to Vienna, from this side, is truly grand. On the left side, the vast Danube, on the right, the superb Schönbrunn, and before your eyes the Imperial city; from the midst of which the venerable dome and spire of St. Stephen rises, guarded, as it were, by the proud double eagle. You pass the lines, which surround all the suburbs.

The houses are generally two stories high, and with the gardens, their white, yellow, or green painted walls, nearly resemble English country mansions. They increase, as you advance towards the city, to three stories, and terminate in a huge palace, or a church, which fronts the city. Between this and the suburbs which surround it, at the distance of about six hundred yards, numerous alleys convey you to any of the twelve gates, only eight, however, of which are open. You enter the Burgtor, whose adjoining ramparts, dismantled by Napoleon's orders, have been laid out in gardens.

There is not in Vienna, as in Paris, the leading hand of a great genius visible, whose architectural beauties are placed with a discerning taste, so as to produce a fine effect.

The Imperial Burg, tainted with the gray hue of age, contrasts strangely with the splendid and modern apartments of the Imperial Chancellery; but it convinces you at once of that Imperial pride which prefers a stately ancient residence to a more splendid modern one. The interior is magnificent, and the pomp and taste of nearly six centuries are here blended in the different dresses and exhibitions of this splendid court. A guard of grenadiers on the left hand, with four mounted cannons, show you that you are before the entrance of the Emperor's apartments. A double flight of stairs leads hence to a noble staircase from this to the first guardroom, occupied by the German and Hungarian guards; the former dressed as Austrian majors of the infantry, in white coats with red cuffs and collars, three-cornered hats trimmed with gold lace. The Hungarian is the Hussar dress, with their tiger skin *calpacs* glittering with gold and embroidery, without doubt the most splendid guard in the world. Their number is fifty, all of them Hungarian noblemen, who bear the rank of premier lieutenants. Their captain is Prince Esterházy. From this dazzling apartment you enter into that of a sort of Pensionaires, dressed in yellow and black mixture, of the old Spanish and German costume. From this you go into the common *Saal*, or audience room. The next apartment is that of the Imperial pages, dressed in red and silver. A few steps farther will bring you to the apartment of the chamberlains, two of whom are always in waiting: they are distinguished by a gold bullion on their back and a golden key. Of the sumptuousness of this court personnel, you may form an idea by the twenty-five body coachmen, fifty body footmen, and twenty-five body servants of the chambers attending his Majesty. The adjoining room is the private cabinet, a simple but costly-furnished chamber with green curtains, in which, leaning with the right hand on a moderate mahogany table, there stands a figure of a middle size, but exceedingly lank, surmounted by an oblong head with a couple of large blue eyes, apparently all openness and sincerity but for a sinister twinkling, long and hollow cheeks, which seem to have ceded all their flesh to the chin, and a pair of thick lips, expressing now and then a good-humored complacency, with his head at times nodding, and again a scowling sullenness. Let your eyes descend on a frame most loosely hung together, legs on which four consorts have scarcely left an ounce of flesh, boots dangling about a pair of equally ill-provided feet — and you have the descendant of nineteen Emperors, and the present Sovereign of Austria. When still archduke, he followed his uncle, the Emperor Joseph, to Hungary. A certain phlegm, and I may be allowed to say everyday manner, made this Emperor exclaim, in a fit of impatience, "That is a good-for-nothing boy, he will spoil everything again," alluding to the reforms Joseph had carried on. The opinion which Prince Kaunitz gave shortly before his death, was little more flattering. "The French Revolution is going to make Europe one large field of battle. I am sorry my country will be the chief party in the contest, will be the loser, and what has been united during five hundred years, will be dissolved."

This prince has been an instrument in the hands of his subjects during his whole reign, not so much from imbecility, as from a certain wily indolence, which, conscious of its own inefficacy, throws itself on others as long as policy and circumstances seem to dictate it. From his accession to the throne in 1792 till 1811, when he fell into the hands of Metternich, he was entirely guided by the leading and binding features of the Austrian monarchy, its powerful oligarchy, and struggled with the French nation with that slow firmness and unceasing pertinacity which no losses of battles, no treachery nor disasters could weary, and which might have been expected from a powerful aristocracy, who considered their interests and their very existence at stake.

During this whole period, when openly betrayed by his generals, as Mack and A⎯⎯⎯g, deserted by his Prussian and Russian allies, after the tremendous disasters at Marengo and Ulm, yet Francis never lost, even for a moment, his phlegm and that indifference, of which it is almost impossible to give an idea. There was hardly any change in his mien or in his favorite occupations — seal wax making, looking after his pigeons, and playing the violin, which he attended to as regularly, when at Vienna, as to his current business. Just as a master, whose servant has broken a dozen of champagne, will tell his butler before dinner, "Now you may look where to get another dozen," so Francis, after the loss of a battle, or capture of an army, would say to his ministers, "Now you may look where you can get an army again." The issue of the sanguinary battle of Marengo roused the spirits of his subjects, and their desire of revenge, wonderfully. The Austrian, Bohemian, and Moravian youths rose unanimously in arms, and offered themselves for the defense of the country. There were among these troops, called the Aufgebot of Prince Charles, six hundred students from the University at Prague, many of whom were noblemen, all of distinguished families. The Emperor was prevailed upon by his brother Charles to review these valiant youths, and to pay them some compliment. The review took place at Budweis in Bohemia, and Francis expressed his satisfaction. "Oh! you look very handsome; I could not have believed it: but I am glad I don't want you. We have now peace, and you may go home again." As a proof of his Imperial satisfaction, he ordered the distribution of a new-coined florin (two shillings) to each of these gentlemen. The incensed youths threw this acknowledgment of high favor unanimously into the river. It is difficult to conceive how by so little encouragement, and with so few shining qualities as a sovereign, Francis could have carried on a war such as that of 1809. It is certainly the most splendid period in the modern history of Austria, and shows more than anything what this power may perform when roused and properly managed. More than 60,000 soldiers were raised, trained, and led to the field of battle by the nobility alone of the different provinces, and at their own expense. Immense were their exertions, as well as those of the people in general. The ornaments of the churches; the plate of the noblemen; the trinkets of the wealthy; the silver spoons and forks of the middle classes, all went the same way, to defray the expenses of this war, without murmuring or repining. The battle of Regensburg, far from damping the spirits of the people, only augmented their exertions, which were crowned by the glorious battle at Aspern. It inspired the whole empire with an incredible enthusiasm, and Francis went even so far as to acknowledge the exertions of his army in an address of thanks. The battle of Wagram succeeded. The plan of the Archduke Charles for this battle is well known. With the united armies under his own and Archduke John's commands, he resolved to enfold Napoleon and to crush him. The contest began with fury on both sides. The right wing under Charles was victorious, and kept advancing. The left, which was to be joined by Archduke John, was hard pressed and retreating. Every eye was anxiously turned towards the road to Pressburg, whence Prince John was expected. Francis, then at his headquarters at Wolkersdorf, sat quietly at his dinner, when one of the adjutants came with the bad tidings of the non-appearance of Archduke John, and the retreat of the army. "Have I not told you," said the Emperor to his Aide-de-camp, B———n D———, rising at the same time, "that John will leave us to fight our battle alone, and that we shall have again to pay the reckoning? Now we may look for the hole which the carpenter has left open!" (Habe ich's nicht gesagt, daß uns Johann wird sitzen lassen, und daß wir wieder die Zeche werden bezahlen müssen. Jetzt können wir schauen, wo der Zimmermann das Loch offen gelassen hat.) So saying, his Majesty rose, and stepped into his calash, with a phlegm which astounded everyone.

Certain hints respecting the secret views of his brother, the Archduke Charles, determined Francis to deprive him of his command immediately after the battle, and to conclude a disadvantageous peace. The same person who gave him these hints, was appointed his Minister of Foreign Affairs. Being on good terms with Napoleon, he wanted neither army nor nobility any longer, and he acknowledged their services in a manner which alone would be sufficient to stifle the most enthusiastic valor. The licenses for trafficking with tobacco and snuff, enjoyed by some thousands of old women and plebeians, were recalled and given to those officers who had distinguished themselves throughout this campaign. The nobility, if they were not entirely cast aside, were at least treated in a manner that damped their spirits more effectually than all their former sacrifices and losses. From the moment Francis put himself into the hands of Metternich, not a trace was to be found of that frankness and uprightness which, notwithstanding the vacillating inexperience of his youth, had guided him through the different stages and storms of his political life. His subserviency to the views of his son-in-law was disgusting even to the latter himself; but poor Napoleon was too little of a courtier to penetrate his father-in-law and his counselor. When at Dresden with his son-in-law, the latter paid him a visit the next day after his arrival. Short and quick as he was in all his doings, he instantly proposed Silesia in exchange for Poland, then in the possession of Austria. Metternich was called from the next room. The discussion grew warmer, and Francis told his minister in German — "Metternich, no! that won't do; I don't want his Silesia; nor will I give up Poland; and tell him that I don't like this way: he will give us today Silesia, and take it in a fortnight, as he does now from the poor d———l the King of Prussia. He has not kept his word and returned to us Trieste and other places as he promised to me."

"What does he say?" asked Napoleon, angry at the broad sounds of the Austrian tongue. "Oh, nothing," said Metternich, with a courteous bow, "but the most sincere assurances of inviolable attachment to your Imperial Majesty." A few hours afterwards, his Austrian Majesty laughed heartily, telling his confidant, "My Metternich is a clever fellow for making an X for a Y;" and with a cunning nod, "I hope we shall succeed." According to this promise of a faithful alliance, Prince Schwarzenberg was sent with the stipulated 30,000 men to Poland, and behaved so valiantly, that from the 500,000 troops who composed the invading French army and their auxiliaries, he alone returned with his 30,000 men, having, in reality, more assisted the Russians than Napoleon.

Never was there a monarch engaged in a more important question than Francis in the year 1813. When Alexander and Frederick William arrived at Prague, their armies were beaten at Grossbeeren and Bautzen; their armaments scarcely begun; the fortresses of the whole of Prussia, even Danzig, in the hands of Napoleon, to whose victorious army of 150,000 they could not oppose 50,000. Favorable as the season was, Prussia and Russia must have fallen. On the other hand, with the Duke of Wellington advancing in Spain, Francis dissatisfied, Germany fomenting and anxious to break its yoke, Napoleon's situation was not less desperate, and he who would have disdained under any other circumstances to stoop to Francis, submitted. The fate of Europe lay in his hands. Whatever party he chose, if he acted on firm principles, it was almost impossible not to bind with the strongest ties of a lasting gratitude to him, and to his empire. It was in his power to show himself, his family, and his empire, as the bulwark of Europe, and the interest of everyone to see its strength undiminished.

Nothing more was necessary than to pursue with England the path which he trod for twenty years. England itself would have honored him as a noble ally, the Bourbons of France and Prussia as their savior, Russia as a firm empire. Francis had a man who was honest and firm enough to propose this course to his master; it was the excellent, but too little known, Generalissimo of the Allied armies, Prince Schwarzenberg. His bad genius prevailed, and he gave himself up to Metternich and his guidance, and then became, from the head of the Alliance, the instrument of Alexander. This monarch played a submissive part to Francis till Paris was conquered; then he thought it no longer necessary, and Napoleon was dethroned before Francis dreamed of it. Russia earned, in fact, the whole fruit of these wars; crushed a powerful rival, exhausted its neighbors and allies, England, Austria, and Prussia, beyond imagination, and thus prepared its way to universal monarchy. Thus we see Francis, who duped his son-in-law, sacrificed his child and grandchild, was duped in the same manner by Alexander, but not pitied; for Philip of Macedon's saying at Olympia will always stand good. As he had now lost every security against the encroachments of Russia, his minister, always ready in expedients, drew up the Holy Alliance. Alexander, who laughed with his ministers in his heart at the folly of an eternal Holy Alliance, found, however, this plaything useful and put himself at the head of it. Francis is not fond of John Bull, whose sturdy and refractory temper corresponds so ill with his notions of respect due to his Imperial dignity; and while Alexander and Frederick William were going to pay their respects to this omnipotent personage, he went home to make preparation for the reception of his guests in that style of *Saus and Braus* for which the German princes are so justly celebrated.

There is certainly nothing more ungenerous than to see a monarch with his brother sovereigns feasting for six months at the expense of a people exhausted by a twenty-five years' war; but his Majesty was never much troubled with scruples of delicacy. On the contrary, the unexpected success in his plans, and the hoped-for extension of his dominions, filled him with a pride which forthwith manifested itself in new court dresses, in splendid carriages, and in the reform of the whole pageantry at the expense of several millions. He himself grew stern, and his dictates were delivered in the characteristic expression, "I will." — Even his own subjects felt this change, and though far from expressing their discontent, not all of them concurred in his predilections for unlimited power. The first who spoke were the Tyrolese. There is in these mountaineers a simplicity, a strength of mind, a true loftiness which elevates them far above the modern Swiss. When Andreas Hofer, a name whose sound elicits tears from every Tyrolian eye, was in Innsbruck, after the glorious defeat of the Bavarians at Sterzingen, the students with the inhabitants assembled before his hotel to bring him, as they said, a serenade.

A deputation went in to inform Hofer of their intention. Hofer stepped out, uncovered his head, and addressed the multitude. "Hear, my beloved countrymen. This is not a time for vain glory. Do not let us sing and play the fiddle, but let us fall on our knees and pray for strength in our desperate struggle;" and, his rosary in his hand, he knelt down, and the assembled thousands with him. Never was there, perhaps, a prayer more fervent or more sincere.

The distant thunder of the cannon, which they heard a few hours afterwards, told them that Hofer was again engaged with the enemy. The Bavarians treated the Tyrolese, after their return to obedience, in a generous manner, and tried by every means to reconcile them. When they fell again into the hands of Austria, contributions, taxes, a host of *douaniers*, and the conscription, made them aware of their mistake, and feel the difference between the Bavarian scepter and the Austrian yoke. To pray for an alleviation and their ancient constitution, a deputation consisting of two prelates, two lords, and two commoners, went over to Vienna. These latter still exercise their privilege to address the Emperor in the first person. Francis received them frowning, the mere name of a constitution being, indeed, the only thing which will affect his phlegm.

The answer which he gave them is worth preserving in the constitutional annals of the present times. "So you want a constitution, do ye?" — "Yes, Francis," answered the two commons with a firm voice, while the lords and prelates bowed. — "Now look ye," replied he, "I don't care; I will give you a constitution; but let me tell you, the soldiers are mine, and if I want money, I shan't ask you twice; and as to your tongues, I would advise you not to let them go too far:" to which Imperial *impromptu* the Tyrolese replied, "If thou thinkest so, we are better without any." — "I think so myself," concluded his Majesty.

Of a rather more serious nature were the petitions or rather demands of the Hungarians. Francis was never a favorite with this lofty nation of noblemen. His plainness and common manner, so much admired among his German subjects, and so well calculated to make them forget taxes and oppression, they do not hesitate to call vulgarity. With a growing discontent, since the reign of Joseph II, they watched over their rights, joined but coldly in the wars of Austria, and were even, during the eventful period of 1809, with difficulty prevailed upon to furnish more troops than their stipulated contingent. Though they refused the offer of Napoleon to choose a king of their own, yet to see their king subservient, as Francis showed himself to Napoleon, and then to act so perfidious a part, mortified them exceedingly. During the time of the wars, and while the Emperor was guided by the counsels and influence of their nobility, they overlooked the encroachments attempted at different times, and even the suspension of the sittings of their Diet. Repeated petitions were presented, yet they never complained loudly. Things have, however, changed and assumed a rather serious aspect, since Metternich was placed at the head of affairs. Repeated encroachments on their constitution, and, above all, the engrossing of the sole power, formerly possessed by the whole body of the aristocracy, by their sovereign, roused the indignation of this nation, in a manner which alarmed even the phlegm of his Majesty. Francis himself is little fond of his lofty Hungarians, with whom his broad and short way, "I will," would not do; and though he flattered them, apparently in every manner he could, yet he did everything in his power to retaliate on them for their indifference and stubborn neglect of his Imperial dignity. They are excluded from trade with the rest of the Empire, and considered, in fact, as strangers.

Exports and imports are subject to the same duties as coming from a foreign country. His policy, with respect to the Greeks, who confess the same religion with, at least, 4,000,000 of Hungarians, contributed, with the fluctuating value of the depreciated currency, not a little to augment their indignation. The freedom with which they proceed in their parliamentary discussions offended his Majesty more than anything; and when he complained that they were sitting four weeks without deciding anything, one of the Magnates, Count P——, rose and said, "His Majesty has been seated thirty years on the throne of Hungary and has not done anything for us." A certain respect for his age and a habit of obeying during a reign of thirty-four years will keep this nation in proper bounds as long as Francis lives; but his successor will have all the indignities and bad humors, collected during fifty years, to contend with. But even in the rest of the Empire, the German hereditary dominions, everything is not as his Majesty wishes it to be. There is not a monarchy whose interior relations are both so intricate and delicate. The titles of possession by which the House of Austria acquired their dominions, are, with the exception of Austria proper, Italy, and Poland, marriage titles; the ties by which these 20,000,000 were kept in obedience, were not so much military power as affection; the principle of honor and good faith on the part of the subjects; and a certain respect towards the rooted habits of the people; and the establishment of an economical management of the treasures, and honesty on the part of the monarchs.

It was this principle of honor and good faith which saved Ferdinand IV and caused the defeat of the plans of the Duke of Waldstein. The same also roused the Hungarians and saved Maria Theresa. The neglect of respect towards rooted prejudices and old establishments had cost Joseph II nearly his finest kingdom, Hungary. Though the Austrian monarchs never encouraged arts and sciences to a great extent, yet, with the exception of Bohemia, they did not so openly oppress them; and when Ferdinand II did so, he was severely punished for it. They divested the states of several kingdoms of their obnoxious powers, as in Hungary and Bohemia; but in the former the constitution was left entire, in the latter the form, and both kingdoms might have resumed their national independence, without any change in the administration.

There was never a secret police before, and Joseph II being informed of a placard fixed on the castle walls, rather too high to be legible, caused it to be placed under the very eyes of his subjects. The Government itself was far from being a despotic one. The provincial tribunals, with their governors at their head, represented the sovereign, appointed their respective officers, who were confirmed by the Emperor, and exercised under him a proper authority. The courts of justice were entirely independent. The universities, colleges, and gymnasiums had, till 1811, a shadow left of their own jurisdiction, under the superintendence of the provincial Government; which, small as the influence was which it exercised, flattered the pride of the nations. Maria Theresa had recourse to the church treasures during the Seven Years' War, but refunded this loan most religiously. The taxes were insignificant, comparatively with those of other countries, and those raised during a war were reduced as soon as it was over. There was throughout an honesty, a good faith, a paternal hand visible, which if it inflicted wounds, also cured them. It became a general axiom, *Bella gerant alii, tu, felix Austria, nube.* Though the Austrian monarchy kept not pace with the rest of the world, yet its nations were not unhappy: though it was the happiness of still life. Since the year 1811, the Emperor, they say, has broken his Imperial word of honor not less than twenty times, and not kept his promise a single time. Notwithstanding a repeated bankruptcy, which reduced the paper currency, at first to a fifth and then to a third, the Austrians have still only paper currency, which, in spite of the appellation (metaliquis), has only a paper value. "The taxes," they say, "which were, as the Emperor promised, to be reduced after the war, continue in the same manner, and more oppressive than ever." In trade there is an absolute stagnation, as the strange policy of Metternich closes the roads to Hungary and Germany. The treasures of their churches, which the Emperor promised to restore in the most solemn manner, are gone forever; they see themselves watched by thousands of spies, and, to open their eyes more completely, they see the Turks, whom they call the Erbfeind, (the hereditary enemies of Christendom) favored and protected against Christian brethren, in spite of the religious profession and devotedness of his Majesty. Where personal affection and religious faith are the only ties which bind nations to their sovereign, as is the case in Austria, it is certainly not a trifling matter to see all these things so grossly violated. The successor of Francis will execrate the blindness with which this ill-fated monarch chimes in with the blighting, withering policy of his prime minister. It is a painful idea to be thought more *sot* than one really is, but to be made more *sot*, and to feel the degrading hand, and not to hate it, is impossible. To affirm that the nations which compose the Austrian Empire are insensible or indifferent about their treatment, shows a want of understanding. We must not judge of the state of this Empire from the Austrian observers, or tourists, who have gathered their information in some taverns, watched by a dozen spies.

The Bohemians, Moravians, Hungarians, and Poles, are not Englishmen, nor even Germans, in point of enlightened information; but they have infinitely more strength of mind and national feeling than the latter. The silence which reigns throughout Austria is compulsory; but the "*aqua tofana*" of Metternich's system is too complicated not to excite the attention and the indignation even of the most stolid human being. To reduce the youth of an empire of thirty millions to that low degree of idiotism which befits the views of his Majesty, it is not sufficient to write schoolbooks in Vienna, by Messrs. Frint and Co., and to send them to the different universities and colleges: there have been, and still are, men upright and learned; they must be removed and replaced by faithful slaves. This has been done with the universities of Prague, Vienna, Olmütz, Laibach, etc. Of the horror which this measure spread all over the Empire we know nothing; but it will never be forgotten. The consequence was the revolt of these universities and the sending of the youths to the regiments on the Banat. It has made the Emperor Francis more hated than all his taxes. To insure a complete obedience, the Emperor has divested the provincial Governments and tribunals of their authority. The sole and absolute power is now in his own and his minister's hands, and the Governments are not allowed to dispose of a sum above two and a half pounds sterling; but, instead of concentrating business and of insuring obedience, this measure had no other end than to disaffect the nobility and the provinces, and to create abuses; notwithstanding new hosts of fresh officers, and a confusion of which it is almost impossible to form a competent idea. There were, during my stay at Vienna, not less than 6000 *exhibits*, as they are called, laid up for the Imperial decision.

The reasoning even of the peasants is simple but true. They are still able to read, and to peruse the Imperial patents and decrees, of which, they say, not one has kept its promises. Though they are not financiers, and are ignorant of Metternich's shameful bartering with Rothschild and his brethren, yet they feel the effects of it: "The silver," the simple Austrian says, "of our churches is gone. We pay still the taxes which were levied only for the term of two years. Our currency changes every day — every hour: we have now a florin in our hands; tomorrow, perhaps, three-quarters; and after tomorrow, a third." As to the Austrian proper, he loves his Emperor with that heartiness with which the German tribes are attached to their princes and their faults; but still he will tell you, "Yes, our Franzl is a good man; but he has belied us very often: and if I were he," turning his neck with a cunning sudden jerk, "I would place Metternich still higher — on the gallows!" In Moravia, where his familiarity is already less known, and where they appreciate his Majesty more from the tenor of his decrees, they will speak very indifferently, or not at all of him; and in Bohemia, the beloved Franzl has lost all credit. They dare not call him names, but they think and hate him as a downright faithless tyrant.

Francis is well aware what is going on, and so are the principal characters; and therefore the thousands of secret spies, watching, not the foreigners, but his own subjects; his repeated visits to Bohemia and Hungary; his remission of the outstanding taxes and contributions to both kingdoms; and his endeavors to secure the succession to his beloved son Archduke Francis Charles, — whom he thinks more able to master the impending storm than the Crown Prince: — but, with all his endeavors, he will not be able to lay the rising ghost. Silent, deep, but embittered, this people go on: Francis has instructed them in the art of dissimulation and treachery, and the successor of Francis will reap the fruits of it. The deep-rooted habit of obeying, a certain reverence towards his age, and, above all, the well-known omniscience of the Emperor and his designs, will keep them in obedience as long as he lives, and as long as he is able to pay his spies and his army of officers; but the load of the public debt, the financial confusion, is too great, and the resources of the German hereditary dominions are too exhausted, to permit a long continuance of this system. Opposed as the Hungarians are with their whole and unexhausted strength, and only waiting for the favorable moment, they will raise the standard of opposition and the rest will follow. The ties of honor and good faith which bound the Austrian subjects to their Emperor are entirely broken, and the death of Francis will disclose scenes of which we never dreamed.

Francis is thought to be a mere instrument in the hands of Metternich. This is not the case. It is a similarity of characters and views which exists between himself and his prime minister; he has found out his man, and therefore he adopts his measures and adheres to them. That baneful offspring of a bad conscience, the secret police, is entirely in his hands: he is the chief director of it, and it forms great part of the immense load which lies on his shoulders. So well known is his fondness for secret information, that the vilest of his subjects, who would not dare to pass the threshold of a respectable citizen, approaches, unhesitatingly, his Majesty, provided he brings this venomous stuff. This species of information extends over his whole Empire — the cottage of the peasant, the dwelling of the citizen, the tavern of the landlord, the palace of the nobleman: no place is exempt from his hirelings. He keeps a regular account of his civil, military, and ecclesiastical officers and dignitaries, from the governor down to the clerk. His excellent memory assists him a great deal. According to these secret informations, his officers are nominated. Attachment to his Imperial person is the first requisite, which is always expressed as the reason of the appointment in the diploma.[6]

Of the 60,000 public officers, he himself nominates the principal ministers, presidents, governors, counselors, assessors, directors; as well as generals, colonels, archbishops, bishops, and canons — and all the directors and professors of universities and colleges. In case of a vacancy, the department in which it happens proposes three members. Their merits are weighed according to the prevalent notions, and they are laid before the higher tribunal; there they are again investigated, and either confirmed or changed; and finally laid before the Emperor. Till the year 1816, the Emperor generally chose the first proposed: an exception was a thing unheard of. This is, of course, changed at present. If he has the necessary information respecting the proposed candidates, he appoints one of them to the vacancy; if not, he sends for secret information into the province, where the officer to be appointed lives. If the tidings respecting the public and private character of the individual do not answer the views of his Majesty, one of his ready kept favorites is nominated to the vacancy. The number of these public officers is infinite, and certainly three times greater than that of any other country, owing to the tedious and even ridiculous manner in which public business is carried on. Not an old bench in a schoolroom can be repaired 800 miles from the capital, without its being approved of by the Captain of the Circle, an account sent from thence to the Government of the province, then to the Aulic Tribunal, farther on to the State Council, which lays it before his Majesty. This egregious manner of doing business has caused such an immense number of writings and writers, or public officers, as amount to a large army. Every one of his subjects is of course anxious to share the public money, and this zeal has seconded the expected subserviency and anxiety to comply with the wishes of the Emperor. Francis may be said to have trained his subjects, during the thirty-four years of his reign, to a blind obedience, which has absorbed principle, honor, and all noble sentiments. One is really horror-struck at the sight of the moral havoc caused by the short-sighted simplicity of a prince who, in order to

---

[6] Out of regard to his sincere attachment to our imperial person, H— is hereby appointed to this office, etc.

bear down all dispute of his right and supremacy, has, in fact, overturned honor, morality, religion, and principles. Right is in Austria what pleases the Emperor — his will; wrong, what displeases him.

If the Austrians have not yet become what, if this system should continue ten years longer, they must necessarily be, the vilest and most perfidious people on the face of the earth, it is certainly not the fault of Francis. The education of the youth, public stations, secret policy, everything combines here, to produce political and moral degradation. And this system of degradation he carries on in that plain, coarse, and downright matter-of-fact manner with which a cross master disposes of his house affairs. Compared with the roughness with which Francis handles his subjects by the mere plainness of his manner, the tyranny of Napoleon was a trifle. He incarcerates bishops, as well as princes and counts, just as he pleases; and should his students murmur or rise against their professors, they are sent as private soldiers to the frontiers of Turkey — all in the most parental manner. There is in this prince a strange mixture of unassuming simplicity and of despotic haughtiness, of a truly Jesuitical craftiness with an apparent frankness, of the coarsest and most ungrateful egotism with an apparently kind-hearted indulgence. If you see him driving his old-fashioned, green calash and two, dressed in a brown, shabby cabotte with a corresponding hat, nodding friendly to his right and left, or good-humoredly speaking to his Grand Chamberlain, Count Wrbna, you would think it impossible that in him there is the least pride. Again, when you see sovereigns and princes approaching him with that awe and shyness which mark a decided distrust, and he himself just as plain, even as gross, as if he spoke to the least of his subjects, you feel convinced that there is occasion for being on your guard against an openness which might send you in the plainest way into the dungeons of Munkatsch, Komorn, or Spielberg. He is certainly not a hypocrite, but there is a wiliness and an innate deceit in him, which baffles the keenest eye and really deceived Napoleon. Even his own family trust him little; and though his intercourse with them is plain, and they mix on familiar terms, yet they always keep their distance. Neither his brother nor the Crown Prince is allowed the least interference in public business, except what is allotted to them.

Of his brothers, he likes the Archduke Rainer, Vice-King of Italy, best; of Charles he is jealous; John is too learned for him; the Palatine too impetuous. When this latter prince requested his permission to marry his present (third) wife, the Emperor replied to him, half frowning: "You may take her; but I shall myself pray for her long life, for I presume your next would be a Jewess." Though he is very fond of his Empress, and is frequently heard saying, "Now I am happy!" yet she has no political influence. When he saw her first, he whispered to his Grand Chamberlain, "That is one who will stand a *puff.* I am glad of it. I shall not have a burial again in a fortnight."

He rises commonly at six o'clock, takes breakfast an hour afterwards, and transacts public business till one o'clock, or gives public audiences. At two o'clock he takes a ride, sometimes with his Empress, but oftener with his favorite Grand Chamberlain, the excellent Count Wrbna, or his aide-de-camp, Baron Kutschera. At four o'clock he dines, commonly on five dishes with a dessert: his beverage is water and a liqueur tumbler filled with Tokay.(N-11) After dinner he takes a peep at his plants in the Paradise Garden; or looks whether any of his pigeons have strayed away or have been captured, a circumstance which makes him always angry; and at six o'clock he takes coffee, made in the new Imperial Garden Pavilion by the Empress herself, who, dressed in a plain suit, delights to be cook and landlady in person. The time till supper is filled out with *térzettos,* which he performs on the violin with his favorite aide-de-camp, Baron K———a, and another nobleman or prince. As father of a family, he deserves praise: there is not a more decent and respectable family in the Empire than his own. Besides the higher branches of education, every member of it is obliged to learn a mechanic occupation; and the Archdukes are carpenters and cabinetmakers, and the Crown Prince himself a weaver. Gallantries are entirely excluded: and a celebrated beauty who from an opposite box in the Imperial Theater had the audacity to wish his son-in-law, the Prince of S———o, a good evening, was sent to prison, and the prince himself severely reprimanded. His second son, Francis Charles, is his favorite, a clever young man, of a prepossessing appearance. He is universally spoken of as his successor. Whether this violation of the Pragmatic Sanction, even caused by the absolute stupidity of the Crown Prince, would not be productive of even more serious consequences than the reign of the latter, we doubt very much. Hungary is absolutely against this; and this alone is an impediment which never can nor will be overcome.

Of all the members of his family, the Duke of Reichstadt experiences the most marked tenderness. It seems as if he wished to obliterate the wrong he had inflicted on the father by his double-dealing. He is, indeed, an interesting youth, beautifully formed, with the countenance and the fine-cut lips of his father, and the blue eyes of his mother. One cannot see this blooming youth, with his inexpressible tint of melancholy and thoughtfulness, without a deep emotion. He has not that marked plain and familiar ease of the Austrian princes, who seem to be everywhere at home; but his demeanor is more dignified and noble in the extreme. Two Prussian officers arrived with us at Schönbrunn, his residence, and wished to be introduced to him. His Lord Chamberlain was just refusing their indelicate demand, in rather an derogatory manner, when the Prince stepped out from his apartments and advanced towards the grand staircase before the palace, to take a ride with his governor. He stopped awhile before the two officers, his eyes fixed; describing at the same time figures on the ground. At last, casting a significant glance at them, *"Des Prussiens?"* demanded he; and turning gracefully aside, he went down to mount his horse.

It is an Arabian steed, a present from his grandfather, and he strides it with a nobleness which gives the promise of as good horsemanship as that for which his father was so celebrated. We saw him some time after at the head of his *escadron*, who almost adore him; and he commanded with a precision and a military eye, which prognosticate a future general. He is, by virtue of an Imperial decree, proprietor of the eight domains of the Grand Duke of Tuscany, in Bohemia, with an income of above £20,000 sterling: a greater revenue than is enjoyed by any of the Imperial princes, the Archduke Charles excepted. His title is Duke of Reichstadt. He is addressed *"Euere Durchlaucht,"(Votre Altesse.)* His rank is immediately after that of the princes of the reigning house, the Austrian family of Este and Tuscany. His court establishment is the same with the Imperial princes: he has his *Obersthofmeister,* his Lord Chamberlain, aids-decamp, and a corresponding inferior household. In possession, as he is, of a large fortune, his destination will depend on his talents and on his inclination.

CHAPTER VI

The Austrian Chancellor of State, Prince Metternich.

NEVER has there been a man more detested and dreaded than Metternich. From the Baltic to the Pyrenees, from the boundaries of Turkey to the borders of Holland, there is but one voice heard respecting this Minister — that of execration. As he was the chief instrument in the new modeling of the present form of Europe, the author and the mainspring of the Holy Alliance, that embryo of great events, his character and policy deserve our impartial investigation. Metternich is descended from one of the ancient but impoverished German families, which gave to this country their spiritual princes. A subtle management of affairs at the Congress of Rastatt, where he represented the Counts of Westphalia, brought him under the notice of the Emperor of Austria; and he entered his service as Ambassador to the Court of Dresden. In the year 1806, he was appointed Ambassador to the French Court. Napoleon had just at this time relaxed from his rigor against the ancient French nobility, and they gathered round him in considerable numbers. With a free passport to the coteries of these families, from which, of course, all the illegitimate members of the newly-created nobility were excluded, Metternich glided with that insinuating suavity and graceful demeanor, for which he is so justly celebrated, not only into the secrets and the *chronique scandaleuse* of the French court, but even into the favor of the leading characters, and of Napoleon himself. It was here he imbibed that deep knowledge of Napoleon's character and penetrated those secrets which enabled him to perform, a few years afterwards, the political and diplomatic dramas at Dresden and Prague. In 1810, he was appointed Minister of Foreign Affairs in the place of Count Stadion. How he succeeded to direct the attention of Napoleon to the Princess Maria Louisa; how Prince Schwarzenberg, his successor, managed this business; and how it finally ended; the wise reader will have a key to, in what has been said. Metternich himself disposed the Princess to accept of Napoleon's offer, and conducted her to Paris. Several hints respecting a reward for his services were not understood by Napoleon. We know Metternich's character and how he made up for the disappointment at a subsequent more favorable opportunity.

This failure, however, contributed not a little to facilitate the insinuations of the Russian Autocrat, to whom he was attached since 1806, from a certain similarity of character, such as is consistent with an autocrat and a courtier. The deep secrecy in which Metternich involved the plans of Austria, during the French campaign of Russia, and even during the Congress at Prague, is considered as the *chef-d'œuvre* of his diplomatic genius. Metternich knew the citizen-like notions of Napoleon respecting his matrimony with Maria Louisa, and it was not a great matter of difficulty to keep him, during the Congress at Dresden, the invasion, and the succeeding armistice, and the Congress at Prague, in suspense, — till the Austrian armies were in array, and the mask could safely be thrown off. Napoleon's pride and unbridled selfishness, which made it impossible for him to see with other eyes than his own, contributed more to his deception and subsequent ruin than even Metternich himself. It was this offended pride which made him recall his ambassador, Count Narbonne, the only one who penetrated the designs of Metternich. The substitution was most unfortunate: — the proud, impetuous Caulaincourt, a slave to his master and blind to everything which was going on in Prague, except horses. Fate retributed fully this deception. Metternich became the instrument of Alexander; and if he was not his dupe, he was something still worse. It was he, through whom the Russian Autocrat prevailed upon Schwarzenberg to risk the advance towards Paris and thus to terminate the war with a single blow. Alexander managed the parties in Paris so well, that the news of the taking of this capital and the dethronement of Napoleon arrived at the same time at the headquarters of the Austrian Empire.

When Metternich showed the plan of the Holy Alliance to P———— W————y, the latter replied, *"Mais, mon Prince, cela offensera."* *"Des fantaisies!"* was the answer of Metternich. In this point, however, Metternich is mistaken: he certainly knows sovereigns and courtiers better than any man living, but not the people; and in the same manner as Napoleon ruined himself from want of proper knowledge of the legitimate characters and their hangers-on, so the Holy Alliance and Metternich's consequent adherence to its principles has done Austria more harm than all the perfidy of this minister has done good. Metternich's exterior is graceful, though not without a sort of effeminacy. A broad forehead, a fine nose, blue well-formed eyes, an agreeable mouth, which has always a smile at his command, with a well-shaped figure, are the outlines of the Austrian Prime Minister. No man turns these gifts to better advantage. With a grace, a *sans gêne*, not in the least encumbered by any of those drawbacks, religion, morality, or principle — he will entertain a circle of fifty and more persons in the most charming manner — enter into dissipation and the follies of his equals and superiors: but, at the same time, while administering to the pleasures and vices of others, will form his schemes on their frailties and hobbyhorses. In the art of penetrating the weak sides of his superiors, and, what is still more, of making himself necessary to their frailties, he is absolutely a master. It was in the midst of revelry, during the Congress at Vienna, that the R———n E———r grew tired of these fastidious bacchanalia. The Prime Minister was, as may be thought, embarrassed not a little. It might have deprived him of A———r's presence — of all the fruits of his fine-spun combinations. Intimately acquainted with the amiable weak side of his new patron, he perceived that then a stimulating *divertissement* would do very well. The gorgeous tournaments, balls, and dinners, were all at once superseded by *petites soirées* given by Metternich, at which the beautiful P———p of S———g, a born P———ss de Cl———g, was the queen. The family of the Princess, however, saw the affair in another light, and the contrivance failed of success. With the same ingenuity as she was drawn into these *petites familiarités*, she extricated herself and withdrew from Vienna to F———g. A———r followed: and the fair fugitive was once more compelled to fly before the would-be conqueror. Metternich availed himself in the interim of the time and tide; and it was principally owing to the transcendent charms of this talisman, which drew A———r to the subsequent tedious Congresses at Troppau and Laibach.

Austria is, no doubt, indebted to Metternich and his stratagems for its aggrandizement and its geographical *arrondissement*. Venice, Milan, and, above all, the Tyrol, Salzburg, and the territory which he prevailed on Bavaria, in the most specious terms, to return, are important acquisitions. This empire constitutes now a compact body of kingdoms and provinces with more than thirty millions of inhabitants and a considerable seacoast; — a monarchy which, if its interests were properly understood and managed, might prove a match against the most powerful on the continent of Europe. Why the same minister has suffered, nay contributed, to lay Austria at the mercy of Russia, and put it in the power of the latter to bring her armies, after a successful battle, before the gates of Vienna, and to separate the empire into two parts, it would be difficult to explain unless we refer to note (N-12).

The position of this Empire becomes, with respect to Russia, indeed, every day more and more critical. The latter Government has, since the times of Catherine I, availed itself of the religious ties which exist between the Russians and the Turkish provinces, Moldavia, Walachia, Serbia, Bosnia, Bulgaria, Croatia, and Dalmatia, to detach them gradually from the Ottoman Porte. They are now almost openly governed by Russian consuls; the crescent is but a shadow there, and the natives are in fact more Russian than Turkish subjects. Sooner or later these provinces will be annexed to the Russian colossus, and form with Greece, the natural allies of Russia, a front which chains Austria, faces the whole of Europe, and commands the Mediterranean. There is no doubt as to what would then become of Hungary,(N-13) Transylvania, and the Austrian Croatia and Dalmatia.

The Hungarians themselves, or, as they are called, the Magyars, are the thirteenth tribe of the Finnish nation, twelve smaller tribes of which reside in Russia. More than four millions of Hungarians are of the Greek confession. Indifferent as they already are to the House of Austria, they would be, in a short time, drawn over to the Russian interest, and the fate of this kingdom, and of Austria itself, could be no longer doubtful: they would be joined to the Russian Empire. To mend his policy, Metternich favors the Turks, and takes a lively interest in their present new modeling — during the lifetime of Alexander in a clandestine, and since his death, in an open way, by demonstrations and armies sent to Poland.

That the Austrian nations desire their constitutions as much as any other people, no person will dispute, from what we see going on in Hungary, Bohemia, Italy, and the Tyrol. But, besides that constitutions are an utter abhorrence to Metternich and his master, these people want their old constitutions. Bohemia wants that granted by Rudolf II; Hungary would disdain to hear of any other constitution than its own; the Tyrol desires its monarchs to deliver to them their coronation oath, sitting on the Ducal Stone in a field near Innsbruck, just as their counts did in the twelfth century; Venice sighs after its Doge; Milan after its dukes. To satisfy and to manage, at the same time, so many different bodies and interests, would require more pliability than even Metternich is master of. The easiest and the shortest way seemed to him that of precluding infection, and, if possible, of destroying bad examples. The King of Naples accordingly is drawn from his capital, and Naples and Piedmont are overrun with Austrian soldiers, and the French sent to Spain. From the same reason, the constitutions of Germany are newly-modeled, so as to make them harmless playthings and inoffensive to their neighbors, the Bohemians and Moravians.

The manner in which Metternich carries his measures into effect is certainly unique. To a perfect knowledge of all the leading characters with whom he has to deal, he unites an acuteness in selecting his instruments, not less astonishing. He has indeed collected a living gallery of Metternichians. His ambassadors are a sufficient proof of this fact. Like an immense spider, he has woven his net over the whole of Europe; has his spies in every capital; is in Portugal with the Miguelites; in Spain, France, and Italy with the aristocrats and priests; and in Constantinople with the Sultan, hand and glove: thus wielding or rather resisting the destinies of Europe more than any other person. As a diplomatist, and as a political intriguer, we may be allowed to say, he stands unrivaled: but there his power ends. Where something more than shifting and intriguing is necessary, his genius fails him. As a statesman — if we call by this name a man who consults the true interests of his prince and of his country, and acts on a great plan — he is very indifferent.

We shall forbear long inquiry as to the best course to be pursued with respect to Austria, and willingly allow that this Empire and its nations are not yet ripe for a constitution. A constitution, whether extorted by the force of arms from a weak prince, or whether the free gift of a sovereign, will sleep and not be properly enjoyed by the nation until the materials for its proper use are ready prepared in it:

— a proportionate division of property and intellectual light. England only made a constant use of its excellent charter, when the feudal power of its barons was broken, property more equally divided, and the nation enlightened. France follows in the same footsteps. Germany has light, but the steps which in Prussia have been taken during the administration of Baron Stein are again in a retrograde movement. The rest of Germany consists of a collection of vast manors belonging to lords, who are called kings and princes; their subjects are little better than tenants. The Austrian Empire presents but immense domains of the nobility and small parcels of land of the peasantry. There is no connecting link between these two extremes of wealth and information, and of poverty and darkness, in a third middle-state. A great statesman, such a one as Chatham-Pitt, Sully, Colbert, or Stein, would have sold the immense domains of the *crown, of the fund of public worship, of the studies, and of the different corporations* to the nation, and thus have created a third order, and the materials for a steady and moral futurity. They would have promoted, at the same time, rational information. The former ministers of France would certainly have pursued a third course, that of a paternal Government, an economical retrenchment of the public expenses, re-establishment of order in the finances, strict justice towards the people, a religious adherence to promises and to public faith, and a successive and gradual improvement. They would have proceeded on the road which Francis pursued, and successfully pursued till 1811. This would, perhaps, have been the course most suitable to the present interest of this vast collection of provinces.

Metternich chooses according to his character, stemming the torrent by moral degradation. The consequences are universal detestation of Austria among the nations of Europe and a shyness and silent hostility, even on the part of other courts, to associate with a policy so absolutely devoid of honor and principle. Metternich now stands alone and deserted, with his policy supported only by his armies, and his spies, and his confederates.

Dazzling as Austria's power and policy may appear in foreign countries, an observing traveler, not entirely excluded from the higher circles, will soon find out that Austria is nearer a crisis than, perhaps, any other country. There will not be a simultaneous rise or a pre-concerted plan to assert popular rights by force of arms; the provinces are too closely watched, and even too much opposed to each other. The Bohemians would not hesitate to march against the Hungarians, the Poles against the Italians, and the Austrians against all of them, even in the present time. But just such a minister, with his withering system, destroying faith, honor, and principle, squandering the treasures of the nation, and crippling the resources of the German hereditary dominions, was destined to pave the road to that very emancipation, which spreads more and more throughout Europe — at a time when the proud Hungarians begin to be tired of farther encroachments and to be ashamed of a policy and of a Government protected only from universal contempt by its power and its intrigues.

Metternich is certainly a man of high talents, his policy is dreadfully consistent, and never has there existed a more dangerous enemy to human freedom; but his knowledge is entirely superficial. He is a very indifferent lawyer and an absolute idiot in financial matters. Indeed, the first step in Austria, its double paper currency, convinces one sufficiently that there is, certainly, not a worse financial management in any country. His acquirements are entirely those of a courtier, in the worst sense of the word. A self-possession, under the most trying and harassing circumstances; a sure and fine tact in judging characters; an ease in gliding into the secrets and the confidence of his superiors; and, above all, an inimitable grace of lying, as they say, with an assurance which it is not in the power of any human being to disconcert — are his principal characteristics. During one of his coteries, or rather courts, which he holds as regularly as the Emperor does his grand and *petit gala* days, he addressed himself to the Bavarian minister in that *apropos* manner for which he is so well known: "Your King seems very fond of liberal ideas?" The ambassador was puzzled, but did not reply. "And of the Greeks too?" No answer. "A little more prudence would do no harm, or his Bavarian Majesty will force us to reprisals not likely to please him. You may inform your sovereign of this."

The new King of Bavaria had, just at this time, introduced several liberal regulations; which, with his open zeal in favor of the Greeks, displeased Metternich extremely. The ambassador thought it his full duty to report these insinuations to his sovereign. The incensed king sends orders to his ambassador to address to Metternich these words: "The King of Bavaria is, as sovereign, bound to no explanation except to God and his conscience, and wishes Prince Metternich to let him alone."

Metternich instantly dispatched a courier to Munich, expressing the utmost concern and astonishment at receiving such a message, as he never had, in any manner, expressed the least opinion respecting the measures of so wise a monarch! At the same time he complained, in bitter terms, of the misrepresentations of the ambassador. This nobleman was, *of course*, wrong; he was recalled, and another sent in his place. Where such a policy is uppermost, an open opposition would be folly. The nobility of the Austrian Empire feel it, and they pay both him and his master in the same manner.

CHAPTER VII

Austrian Aristocracy. – Viennese High Life.

THE Austrian oligarchy is now, if not in a state of disgrace with his Majesty, at least nearly approaching to it; and it may justly say, with the Duke of Ormonde, "that there could not be any whose influence was smaller with kings and ministers." The power which they enjoyed till the year 1811, was that which the possession of two-thirds of the landed property naturally gave them: a paramount influence in the councils of war and the policy of the cabinet, with a proper regard to their interest.

The nobility in this empire formed thus the gradual transition by which the prostration of eastern slavery was linked to the greater freedom of the western world. The Emperor of Austria in his German and Bohemian hereditary dominions is considered an autocrat as well as the Russian; but while the latter may deprive the first family of their rank and domains, the Austrian house, whose founder was himself but a nobleman, and who acquired his possessions not by conquest but by marriage titles and the concurrence of the nobility, is rather checked by them. This is still more the case with Hungary. The present calm state of the Empire was preceded by frequent revolts, in which the highest nobility were engaged. The names of Waldstein, Schlick, Frangipan, etc. are still dreadful recollections to the Imperial family. Such, however, was the influence of these families, that they kept possession of their titles and estates, though the authors of these revolts were punished with death. A prudent management, on the part of the reigning family, has attached them to the Imperial cause; and their interests, blended with that of the House of Austria, are in fact the strongest, and, we may say, the only guarantee for the fidelity of the different kingdoms. The present Emperor, in that thoughtlessness and indifference towards the real state of his Empire, which is the characteristic feature of his life since 1811, has really cast aside this nobility. Their power is now in the hands of Metternich. Whether an army is to be sent to Naples, or the borders of Poland, Metternich decides, as well as on the policy which is to be pursued, and the degree of power which ministers and provincial Governments are to enjoy. They are reduced to a sort of gaudy ornament of the Imperial Court, and instruments with which the pompous splendor and pride of Austria, at home and abroad, is kept up. The consequence of this supremacy was soon and strikingly felt. Hardly was the power, as formerly enjoyed by the whole Austrian oligarchy, viz. by the Hungarian, Bohemian, and German noblemen, engrossed wholly by Metternich, when the Hungarian nobility and nation claimed their rightful constitution, and put themselves in an attitude which little pleased his Majesty, and still less his Prime Minister.

They resumed in fact their constitution, which had slept for a considerable time. While this was done in Hungary, the Bohemian noblemen, who cannot do the same, endeavored gradually to concentrate and to raise the national spirit by those means still left in their power, such as museums, mathematical, technical, and economical schools. The Emperor and his Prime Minister are well aware of this select but dangerous opposition, and of its tendency. They counteract it with the same design and art which characterize the present Austrian cabinet. His son, the Archduke Charles, the exact picture of his father, only more pleasing in his appearance, was sent as Vice-King to Bohemia, both to conciliate and to watch this people. As Metternich keeps in Vienna a school and court for the education and demoralization of the nobility, so there are in every provincial capital one or more families of the highest rank, who have the double part to counteract the opposition as spies of Metternich, and as stimulating leaders to that dissipation and extravagance which is supposed to draw the attention of the nobility from public affairs and serious occupation.(N-14)

Of the three hundred families who constitute the oligarchy of this Empire, there are about a hundred and fifty who in compliance with the wishes of the Emperor, arising partly from jealous policy, partly to give a due lustre to his Imperial headquarters, reside in Vienna. They may be considered as the representatives of the whole nobility, intimately linked together. The foremost among them are the ducal families, about ten in number; among which those of the Liechtensteins, Schwarzenbergs, Lobkowitz, Esterházy,(N-15) and

Czartorysky, distinguish themselves. The heads of these families, or, as they are called, Regents, are born Knights of the Golden Fleece. They have their regular courts; some of them their guards; all their privy and court counselors, etc. They live in a style little inferior to that of the Emperor himself. To give an adequate idea of the wealth of these powerful vassals, it is sufficient to state that Prince Liechtenstein has not less than 720,000 subjects or peasants on his domains, and rides regularly from his two dukedoms, forming two-thirds of Silesia, through Moravian Austria, a distance of more than a hundred miles on his own estates. Prince Esterházy, though encumbered with immense debts, has still a revenue equal to that of the Kings of Bavaria, Saxony, and Württemberg, taken together.

A medium between sovereign and subject, these families are treated, even by the Emperor, with a deference which a great influence with their countrymen, especially if they are Hungarians, and a vast income ever wring from a sovereign like Francis. Next to them are the ancient Hungarian, Bohemian, and Austrian princes and counts. The aristocracy of Great Britain excepted, there is none at present which has so undisputed a claim to respectability. The names of the Kinskys, Batthyanys, Nadasdys, Starhembergs, Thuns, Sternbergs, and Dietrichsteins, are intimately blended with the most brilliant periods of their national existence; and there is not a single ancient family, which derived its titles in the manner in which not only the Italian, but even many of the French nobility originated.(N-16)

Steadiness and an undeviating adherence to principle deserve esteem, wherever they are to be found; and the pertinacity with which the Austrian oligarchy, so dreaded by Napoleon, advised and fought through the wars against the French demagogues and their leaders, for the maintenance of their rights and principles, is praiseworthy, though their exertions and sacrifices failed of success. They have fought for the same cause, in common with England. It is not a little honorable to them, that during the period when they advised and influenced their sovereign, Austria's honesty was universally acknowledged and respected, its policy trusted; the country itself the asylum of the oppressed and persecuted; while, as soon as their influence was wholly engrossed by Metternich, this power became the abomination of the civilized and moral world. Loyal to their sovereign, the French Revolution acted upon them as a powerful restorative; and the same families, who fifty years ago sent for their linen to Paris, and fancied themselves no noblemen if their wardrobes came not from the same quarter, are now encouraging their countrymen with a patriotism truly laudable.

If you ask, how they bear their present neglect? Just as independent and naturally powerful, but discarded noblemen, will do. There is nothing to be seen or to be heard but urbanity and politeness. They visit regularly (though with many exceptions) the salons of Metternich, and he returns civilly their attentions. No scorn, no hatred, no insinuations regarding an intruding foreigner are to be heard of, save a bitter bill which he has to digest now and then. Anyone who is not a little deeper initiated in the state of things, would suppose all well in the midst of a social warfare conducted in the most polite forms. They act fully as men who know whom they have to deal with: a minister, who with honey on his lips and *aqua tofana* in his heart, distributes the first himself, and the latter through a master, who, in the most familiar and fatherly tone, will tell you the harshest things in the world, and do them too.

The character of the present Government has led many to be unjust towards everything Austrian, or, what is still worse, to confound people and Government. There is as great a difference between the needy German baron, or count, who cringes to the Prime Minister, as exists between the broken fortune hunter and the independent English gentleman. The barometer of respectability of the Austrian oligarchy is, in fact, the greater or less dependence upon and connection with Metternich himself. The zero of moral worthlessness and absolute voidness of principle and honor are the creatures and hands of Metternich: the A⎯⎯ys in P⎯⎯s; the M⎯c⎯h de B⎯⎯n, in F⎯⎯t; the C⎯n⎯, G⎯tz⎯, A⎯⎯g, in Vienna, etc. etc. etc. On the same *niveau*, are the *roués* of Metternich's immediate fraternity; libertines like T⎯f⎯ K⎯⎯z, his own brother-in-law, etc. You will find in their circles, that perfect ease and *sans gêne* of complete political and moral *roués*, who by the *authorité* of sixteen sires, and the *chronique scandaleuse* of the whole of Europe, have got that assurance which will never expose them to a blush or an embarrassment, even if their thoroughly spoiled blood should admit of it. These circles are in fact the true pictures of the

French coteries in the times of Louis XV, stained, however, with a grossness and sensuality which characterize an Austrian debauchee. The sound part of the aristocracy of the Austrian Empire is the national nobility, certainly respectable. It has not that consciousness of real importance and dignity which characterizes the English, if we except the Hungarians. There is a certain shifting bashfulness, or rather timidity, the result of an oppressive system which never permits anyone to raise his head higher than is thought proper: but they are not so frivolous and are better informed than the French. Prince Schwarzenberg was taken from his embassy at Paris, in 1811, to head an army,(N-17) and he commanded the united Austrian, Russian, Prussian, and German armies gloriously. Not less so the Liechtensteins, father and son, the Bubnas, Nostiz, Colloredo, Degenfeld, and Merveldts. It is fair to state that the French, while they execrated the Austrian Government, acknowledged the humanity of those Austrian commanding noblemen at a time when the unceasing emptiness of the Imperial Treasury forced them to imperative measures in the conquered Italian and French provinces. It is easy for us in England to speak of an independent conduct and of a manly resistance to despotism. But come see and feel, and be horror-struck, as you certainly will be: your astonishment will not be the less, how this nobility, standing as they are on the alluvial quicksand of a shifting despotism, and beleaguered with all that train of poisoning machinery, have still left a sense of honor and of principle, to resist, partly open, partly silent, the impending completion of their degradation. There is not a monarchy, whose sovereigns, taken in the whole, have done less for arts and sciences, and the nobility more. We cannot expect from every nobleman the connoisseurship of Goethe, Winckelmann, or Böttiger; but there is no capital where the nobility have among them so many, and such beautiful galleries and museums, as the Austrian nobility. The galleries of Liechtenstein, Esterházy, Lamberg, Schwarzenberg, etc., are of the first order.

 The Austrian artillery is reckoned one of the best in the world. Its officers are learned, solid, and respectable men. This corps is indebted for its present perfection to one of the Liechtensteins, who, at his own expense (and it was immense), undertook and brought about the reform of this corps. He established schools, furnished books and instruments for the whole artillery. The family of Schwarzenberg has an economical and technical establishment at its dukedom, Krumau, in Bohemia, which is supported with a princely liberality. Still more important is the institution of Count Festetics, of which we shall speak at a subsequent period. What the Sternbergs, Kolowrats, Dietrichsteins, Boucquoys, are doing, is well known. The circles of this class of the nobility, even in Vienna, are solid, true imitations of those of the court. As in those too, everything moves as regularly as it did in the time of Leopold I, save a more pompous display of wealth, exhibited in gorgeous show of diamonds and jewels. You will find, in the circles of the nobility, a union of everything delightful, with that stateliness and solidity which blend the ancient grandeur with modern taste. The picture of Austrian high life is less dazzling than the French, but it is more solid. There is less extravagance, less variety than in Paris, but infinitely more reality. It is this steadiness which has preserved their wealth, even through centuries, little impaired by the late disasters; while the French nobility and that of the German states, are generally more or less impoverished.

French is still the favorite language, not so much from an indifference to or scorn of the native German, Hungarian, or Bohemian languages, as from the necessity that is felt to speak a tongue which is not understood by their servants, and does not expose them to the danger of every word being betrayed to the secret police.(N-18)

French manners have, however, lost much of their universal sway, though a tinge of them is still visible throughout Vienna society.

The children of the Austrian nobility are almost universally educated at home. Each family has at least one tutor, generally a lawyer or a divine, who has gone through the course of his studies. This gentleman superintends the education of the young members of the family. While the young ladies take their lessons in religion, writing, drawing, music, or dancing, the youths go through their Latin, or other lessons, under the superintendence of this tutor, or of competent masters, who are sometimes public professors. After the lapse of six months, the youths are publicly examined by the professors of the Government and advanced into a higher class. Even the philosophical course is frequently completed at home in this manner. Though these tutors cannot impart what they have not themselves acquired, yet as they are generally men of learning, and their fortune depends entirely on the progress of their pupils, young noblemen who are not condemned to the mere learning of their lessons by memory, and who have a free literary range, become more thoroughly instructed than the other classes.

A solid family of the high nobility will rise early — between six and eight o'clock — if a ball or a party of the preceding night has not encroached on the morning. A cup or two of coffee, with a small white roll (Semmel), is the usual breakfast, which is taken *en famille*, with the exception of the youths, who breakfast and dine separately with their tutors. The subsequent hours are dedicated to business. The lord is engaged with his privy or court counselor or director of his domains in the current business, which takes from two to three hours: the reading of English, French, and German newspapers.(N-19) The lady is all the while busy in her apartments with the supreme regulations of the household; reading, writing, drawing, and dressing. At twelve o'clock the visiting hours begin. The lady either pays or receives visits, in which, however, her husband seldom participates. Their apartments are generally separate. As they keep separate carriages, the lady takes her ride at two o'clock, either in the company of her husband or of her lady companion, in the Augarten, the Prater, or on the Glacis. At three o'clock dinner is served, attended by the whole family except the youths, who are only permitted to join them on a Sunday, with their tutor.

After dinner the regular ride is taken, and this is followed by the tea party, and fruits at six. The theater or an evening party, for which the dress is again changed, concludes the day. A court gala or a grand party alters, of course, the order of the day. The common hour of set dinners is three. You are invited by cards; and the invitation is sent, according to your rank, either eight or two days before the dinner itself. On entering the mansion of the nobleman, a Swiss will ring the bell — if you are a prince, thrice; if a count or baron, twice; and if a simple nobleman or gentleman, but once. On the staircase, two Jäger (footmen) in rich liveries with broad hangers and epaulettes are waiting. They open the doors. One of them takes your hat and conducts you through an enfilade of splendid rooms to the boudoir of the lady, announcing your name and your character. You are received by her sitting, with a bow, and the four words, "N———, *Sie sind willkommen!*" (N———, you are welcome,) and if you are on terms of intimacy with the family, you are allowed to kiss her hand. You enter into conversation with the gentlemen or ladies present for some minutes. The doors open, and the steward announces dinner. The party generally consists of an equal number of each sex; the gentleman takes his partner, with whom he walks to the dining room. There may be twelve, twenty, or forty guests; but the party is never *thirteen*. The first place at the round table is occupied by the hostess. Each guest has assigned his place, so that a lady is always between two gentlemen, and so *vice versa*. The number of courses after soup is three. The first consists regularly of a haunch of deer, followed by sausages and some stimulating delicacies; boiled beef succeeds, with fricassees, puddings, and fish. The second course consists of roasted pheasants, roe, and fowls: the third, of the dessert. It is fashionable to eat quickly; and the twelve or fifteen dishes which compose the three courses disappear in three quarters of an hour. Carving and helping is, of course, wholly done by the servants. The beverages are exquisite. At the beginning of the dinner, you are asked what sort of wine you prefer. Generally a light Rhine, or Hungarian Buda wine, mixed with water, is the common table beverage. When beef is served, a glass of Malaga is handed round; at the beginning of the second course, old Johannisberger, Rüdesheim, or Steinwein; the third course is accompanied by a tumbler of Champagne; and the dessert itself is crowned by a liqueur glass of the emperor of wines, the spirited Tokay. Toasts or healths are not fashionable, except on public occasions. The whole dinner takes not more than one hour, after which the company rise; each guest pays the usual respect to the hostess and each member of the company with a bow; and the same partners conduct the ladies to the next room, where coffee with liqueurs of Trieste and Italy is served round: the ladies sitting, the gentlemen standing, or as they choose. A conversation of a quarter of an hour ensues; and those not invited for the evening party disappear *incogniti*, without bidding farewell to host or hostess.

An invitation for spending the day with the family is succeeded by a party to the Prater. If you arrive in a hackney coach — viz. if you have no carriage of your own — you ride out in the carriage of the host, who follows that of his wife. In whatever part of the town you may have dined, if it be on a Sunday, you must drive to the Graben or St. Stephen's Church, in order to join the immense line of carriages which runs from thence through the Prater to the town. To go out or to go into this line of not less than three miles in length is impossible, and against the order. Even the Imperial family move slowly on in this corso, behind a hackney coachman or an honest burgher, who drives his cabriolet filled with viands of every sort to this paradise of worldly pleasure. A more imposing, entertaining, and varied sight than this scene cannot be imagined. Close behind the magnificent state coach of the Empress drives a Vienna Zeiselwagen, a sort of ludicrous and favorite conveyance with the lower classes of Vienna. This is a strange specimen of locomotion, loaded with no less strange occupants, and hams, wine flagons, and everything necessary to the Viennese. This is followed again by an elegant phaeton or a light carriage of a Hungarian or Bohemian nobleman with his hussars or Jäger in their gorgeously splendid liveries; while the Emperor, with his worthy grand chamberlain, the Count of Wrbna, drives in a simple unassuming calèche. Behind him you see a foreign ambassador, who is again succeeded by a wealthy Mussulman merchant, a grave, proud, and immovable personage, surrounded by Moors. The whole moves on in a solemn manner and with a magnificence far surpassing every other spectacle of the kind. The alleys to the right and left are filled with horsemen, among whom you may distinguish the Hungarians out of thousands by their noble carriage and by their being very superior riders. The alleys adjoining these two are filled with a well-fed sort of burghers, inferior officers, and tradesmen of the lower classes, who, since their meal, which they took at twelve o'clock and which lasted till two, have again during half-an-hour's walk got an appetite; which may sufficiently account for the 80,000 head of cattle, 67,000 calves, 120,000 lambs, and 72,000 hogs, which are annually swilled down by these 300,000 people, with the assistance of 200,000 pipes of Austrian wine. Unconcerned about the jokes of the fashionables, and even of the Emperor, who takes a sort of pride in the *sans gêne* of his subjects on this occasion, they will sit down on the green grass plots on the lawns and enjoy their hearty *luncheon* with an appetite as if they had not seen any food for two days. On both sides of the fine alleys, circuses and numberless *restaurateurs* with groups of wandering musicians enliven the scenery, while hundreds of merchants' clerks and burghers' sons betake themselves with their paramours to the lawns and the defiles of this beautiful park, in order to get out of sight of the thousands whom fair weather, a good vintage, and, above all, the presence of their dearly beloved *Kaiser*[7], has assembled here; a motley crew of unthinking people, who will fly to arms with the same thoughtlessness as they now sit quietly about their masticating affairs. At six o'clock you return from the promenade with your host to his mansion, where your *fiacre*, in case you have no carriage of your own, is waiting to carry you back to your lodgings. The time between six and eight, is filled up with your toilette for the ensuing ball. A black frock, with silk breeches, stockings of the same color and material, maroquin shoes, and very small golden buckles, are your dress. You repair to the noble entertainer's at eight o'clock. Again the same ringing of the bell, the same reception by the stately Swiss with his gold fringed hat and great coat. Two servants are posted at the foot of the staircase, holding flambeaux, whose flickering light, together with that of a vast lamp, shows you the way to the apartments. Your servant delivers in the antechamber your hat and your *cabotte* or great coat, for which he receives a billet with a number, the same which is affixed to your deposited goods. Again you pass through the enfilade of rooms to the boudoir of the hostess, where you find part of the company already assembled. It is not fashionable to arrive too soon; it is good manners to be too late. The number of the fair dancing candidates will be between thirty and forty, with an equal number of gentlemen. These, with the steady old people who form the whist and *ombre* parties, are assembled in the boudoir and the adjoining rooms. Refreshments, consisting chiefly of fruits, are served up, and before a quarter of an hour elapses, the door of the dancing salon is thrown open, and a profusion of lights, with a powerful salute from the orchestra, fill your eyes and ears and give the signal for the ball. Each party is arranged, and in case you should be an entire stranger, the hostess will introduce you to a fair companion under the auspices of the *marshal de danse*. It is generally the dancing master of the house who holds this office. The partners proceed through the rooms to the salon, which

---

[7] Emperor

with the adjoining apartments is splendidly lighted. The orchestra is placed on a gallery in the background of the salon, consisting of from fifteen to twenty instruments. It opens with a polonaise, followed by a cotillion, which is repeated twice. It was at the ball given by C―――t F―――n that I first saw the beautiful chain dance. On a sudden three powerful notes burst from the orchestra, the signal for this inimitable dance. A pause of about half-a-minute is occupied by the sound of a dozen *castagnettes*, and by the stamping and clapping of the hands of the partners, the signal for the forming of the chain, which with its windings continues unbroken till each gentleman finds his partner. A quick stamping and clapping of the hands, accompanied again by the *castagnettes* from the orchestra and a powerful *accord*, changes the chain into the slow waltz; after which the dance grows quicker and changes into the waltz, and finally into the German or Dutch figure.(N-20) The whole is performed with such inimitable grace, lightness, and absence of every studied air, and with such an elegance as made it indeed one of the finest specimens of a dance I ever witnessed. The ball continues with waltzes and cotillions. The rooms from the dancing salon to the boudoir are occupied with card tables, where whist and *ombre* are played. Splendid buffets with the most exquisite dainties, decorated with a profusion of flowers, spring up from the corners of the adjoining room. At twelve o'clock supper is served. The ladies are led in a polonaise by their partners to the dining room and occupy their chairs according to the cards on which their names are put. A cup of soup is handed round by the servants, after which the usual *fricassées* and roasted varieties of every description follow: the whole in a splendid style. The dance is resumed at one o'clock and continues till three. At this time the crowd begins to thin. The card tables lose their occupants, and the fair dancers are enveloped by their *Jäger* and hussars in their shawls and pelisses, and conveyed, under the superintendence of their papa and mama or an aunt, to the carriages in waiting. Only the intimate acquaintances hold out till four, and these take formal leave of each other; the whole is conducted with the greatest propriety.

    Nothing, however, is more delightful than an evening party in a private circle. You assemble for this occasion immediately after tea, which is regularly taken at six o'clock. Some refreshments, such as pineapples, grapes, etc. are handed round. The whist, quadrille, or *ombre* tables are arranged, and the company sit down to play. During the play a band performs tunes of Mozart's, Weber's, and Rossini's operas; and if there are daughters in the family, whom their friends are coming to see, a dance is arranged before you are aware. There is in every house not only the music master, but at least two or three servants, who are excellent performers. Their rooms not being carpeted, but *parquetted* and polished with wax, are at any time ready for this occasion. It is in these evening parties that the amiable and fascinating character of the high classes of the Austrian Empire shines out in all its charms. The *sans gêne*, the modesty, the true nobleness and simplicity which develop themselves in these circles and occasional dances show that these people are more fitted than any other to enjoy the pleasures of life. They give happiness to their guests and try to make everyone round them happy too. It is impossible for anyone to be more at his ease and at home than in these circles, especially those of the Hungarian nobles. There is no suspicion, no constraint, no fear — nothing of this kind; for the Hungarian feels, and he feels justly, what he is; and that his ancient constitution and personal liberty are not only written on paper, but in the hearts of 10,000,000 of countrymen, fearless of the Emperor and his Metternich. The conversation during dinner turns on every subject: politics, anecdotes, a little of the *chronique scandaleuse* — especially if the Prime Minister is its object, who is treated here with much less ceremony than anywhere else. The anecdotes are mostly relating to the Hungarians themselves; and the noble, unsuspecting, and undissembling character of this most interesting and least of all known nations makes them sometimes commit blunders, which partake very much of the Irish character. Among the many which were dished up, one may suffice. A Hungarian wished to see the prospect of Vienna from the steeple of St. Stephen. Seven hundred steps lead to the second gallery. The turnkey was not at home; and his wife being pregnant, begged him to stay awhile for the return of her husband. "What time," asked the Hungarian, in broken German, and with a significant look at the woman, "will it take?" (meaning: to ascend the steeple) The woman, referring his question to the peculiar state of her corpulence, replied "Five days." "Five days!" exclaimed the Hungarian; "G⎯⎯d d⎯⎯n! In five days I must be in Kecskemet!" and away he flew, glad not to have satisfied his curiosity at five days' expense.

To all these stories our landlord himself, a Hungarian nobleman, listened with the best humor in the world. At last, half-smiling, half-serious, he said: "Why wonder that we are not what we could and should be? On one side we see the Turks, on the other the Austrians: how can it be otherwise? My countryman was right not to look from the steeple top." The joke was well received, except by the stately, but respected and honest colonel of a Hungarian regiment, who was obliged to frown *ex officio*. The Hungarian, however, cares nothing about frowns or smiles, even those of the Emperor. We had an instance of it in our hotel, the Swan.

Young pork with horseradish, and sausages with mustard, and Austrian wine, is a favorite breakfast in Vienna, called *Krenfleisch*. We took it every day and went for this purpose down into the coffee room. It was the very day when public festivities in honor of the restoration of the Emperor were celebrated. Three Hungarian noblemen stalked in, attired in their national costume — crimson-colored corsets with light breeches, hussar boots with tassels of gold bullion, and the pelisse hanging from their shoulders. They took off their sabers and calpacs, and demanded three bottles of Rhine and six of Austrian wine. The humble vintner was rather startled at their demand; but obeyed with an Austrian obsequiousness. "A basin!" said an elderly, stern-looking cavalier. It was brought. "Pour the six bottles of Austrian wine into the basin!" proceeded the same gentleman. It was done. "Put the three bottles of Hungarian wine into the water!" "But, your grace!" replied the trembling vintner, "it is not water; it is the best Bisamberger wine, from the growth of 1811!" "Put it in," said he, "and get you gone!" Every eye was turned towards the bold cavaliers, who, in one of the first hotels, dared thus to show their contempt for Austria. A few minutes afterwards three more joined them; and now they brought out the healths. "Maria Theresa!" was roared out; "*Vivat! Vivat!*" replied the five others. "*To our King!* — *Constitutional!*" added the next. "*Constitutional!*" echoed the other five. The whole was transacted in so serious a manner and with such a dignity, or rather severity, as it is impossible to describe. Not a smile, not a glance at the present guests; alone they sat — alone they spoke; silently they paid for their breakfast and bottles, six of which remained in the basin; and away they went, with that firm, martial, and measured step which shook the tables, tumblers, and windows of the massive building.

It is in the circles of the nobility and the wealthier class of bankers that you will find a certain degree of political freedom and liberty of speech, newspapers, and, as they are called, *"Verbotene Bücher,"* (prohibited books,) in every tongue. There are no political salons of liberals as there are in Paris, except the very highest families of the nobility; where, however, none but the most intimate and confidential friends are admitted: but during a dancing, a dining, or whist party, some couples of gentlemen will loose themselves from the table and step just occasionally into the next room; or a letter received from Paris or London — of course not through the post— will glide from hand to hand in that imperceptible way which Metternich has taught them. That is the way to concert in Austria, measures, plans, and even something more — in the midst of pleasures and gaiety. They are forced into this; as the Emperor, though far from being a Caesar, acts fully on his principle with respect to his subjects — and thinks himself and his family secure as long as his subjects are dancing and singing.

CHAPTER VIII

Public Officers. – Lower Classes. – The City of Vienna considered in an architectural point of view. – Public Worship. – Bias of the Viennese. – Public Institutions. – Austrian Codex. – Medical Science. – Character of its Literati. – Public Journals. – Grillparzer. – Austrian Censorship. – Theaters. – Concluding Remarks.

THERE is not a less popular Government in Europe; one where people, and Government, and its officers, are more virtually separated. There is no class of citizens, in any place, under more restraint than the public functionaries in Vienna.(N-21) They are, in the midst of gaiety and of sensual uproar, tied fast to their writing desks, working, watching, and watched. Vienna is the seat of all the ministries, presidencies, and Aulic tribunals, with several hundreds of Aulic counselors and thousands of inferior *employés*. A Counselor of the Court is an important personage; he has the *referat*, as it is called, of several provinces and kingdoms, with the rank of General-major: — the junior has a pay of 5000, for Austria, a very respectable sum; the elder of 6000 florins, (£500 and £600 sterling), but you will very seldom meet one of them in the circles of high or middle-life, unless he be a nobleman of rank or a bachelor who cares not much about preferment. It is not the mere want of a diploma or of a sufficient income which debars them from these circles, but the well-known pleasure of the Emperor. To intermix in the society or in the pleasures of the gay city would be a sure veto to their advancement. "I want steady men for my Aulic counselors, who visit regularly their bureau and keep hours," replied his Majesty when B———n V———n, a fashionable but able young man, was proposed to him for this station; and, accordingly, his officers are obliged to comply with the hint. The well known G———tz, the author of the Austrian manifestoes and the most important articles in the *Austrian Observer*, was several times proposed to his Majesty for a Counselor of the State, and recommended even by Metternich. "He keeps a mistress," was the Emperor's reply, "and has three children by her" and all these united endeavors were in vain. A Counselor of the State, whose rank is next to that of a minister, is still less to be seen in company. With his appointment to this high station is coupled the silent condition of his retirement from society.

As the Emperor has an exact account of the domestic affairs of his public officers, they cannot move a single step without its being betrayed to the police and to the Emperor; and while he almost forces the high and low classes of his subjects into dissipation and thoughtlessness, he wants his officers to be steady and sober. There was the p⎯⎯⎯hp Prince R⎯⎯⎯y, who entangled the daughter of the Aulic counselor S⎯⎯⎯z into a love affair by means of an ogling correspondence carried on from his windows. The young lady fell love-sick and became silly. The Emperor was informed of it, and the prince summoned before the monarch; "Prince," said the Emperor in a stern voice, "I wish you to understand that the daughters of my Court Counselors are no fit objects for your gallantry. There are plenty in Vienna." The prince had to pay for his intrigue a fine of 15,000 florins, £1500 sterling.

Still severer lies the hand of the Emperor on his soldiers. Disgusting as the military airs of the Prussians are to everyone who looks to something more than military parades and uniforms, yet an Austrian officer is a painful sight. He is kept in a state of obedience approaching degradation. Nothing can be more humble than an Austrian officer in Vienna; even the innate pride of the Hungarian here dies away. The pay of the Austrian officer is a trifle, and if he have not resources of his own, his scanty means exclude him not only from every entertainment, but it is impossible for him to live in a decent style. To make up this insufficiency, his lodgings are paid by the Government at half-price, — of course no landlord is overly-delighted at a military inmate; his meat is delivered to him by the growling butcher, equally at half-price. Theaters and public entertainments are open to him for about a third of the common price; and as all these mending patches were still insufficient, they added to his emoluments fuel and half-a-loaf of commission bread, as it is called; a bread which no English horse would taste.

Vienna is garrisoned by 12,000 men, two regiments of infantry, six battalions of grenadiers, one regiment of artillery, and one of dragoons. Of the infantry, the tall, brawny, and hardy Hungarian grenadiers in their fur bonnets, white jackets, and blue embroidered pantaloons are by far the handsomest. With the exception of the English foot guards, these troops, since the immolation of the Imperial French guard at Waterloo, are without doubt the finest troops in Europe. Neither the Russian nor the Prussian grenadiers can be put in comparison with them. The Austrian infantry are too plain, and rather poorly dressed in white. The dragoons are simple, but extremely noble-looking fellows. Their cocked helmets, tasteful white jackets and pantaloons, high boots with their broadswords and carbines are infinitely superior to the gaudy frippery of the Hungarian hussars. Nothing, however, can be conceived more tasteless than the Austrian artillery uniforms. Their drab-colored jackets and pantaloons, their hats with flaps turned up, one might suppose to be the livery of an impoverished country nobleman, rather than of the virtually best troops in the Austrian army. The bands, however, of all these regiments and troops are superior to everything of their kind. Their music is electrifying beyond description. "If I want to hear music," said Professor W——— in Berlin, at the representation of Spontini's *Olympia*, "I go to Austria. The march of their bands is worth the whole opera."

The character of the great mass of the inhabitants is woefully changed within the last sixteen years. The Viennese were always reputed a sensual, thoughtless sort of beings, content if they could enjoy a drive in their Zeiselwagen into the Prater with their wine and roast meat. But their honesty, kindness, and sincerity were proverbial, and Napoleon himself gave them proofs of his esteem. He left them in the possession of their arms and of their arsenal. Since the year 1811, the 10,000 Naderers or Pinners, as the secret spies of Vienna are called, have done their work. Taken from the lower classes of society, tradesmen, servants, mechanics, prostitutes, they form a confederacy in Vienna which winds like the red silk thread in the British navy through all the intricacies of social life. There is scarcely a word spoken in Vienna which they do not hear. There is no precaution possible, and even if you bring your own servants, if they be not staunch Englishmen with a sufficient stock of pride and contempt towards the Viennese themselves, in less than a fortnight they will involuntarily prove your traitors. The character of the Viennese has become what might be expected under such circumstances. As the Government has taken every care to debar them from serious or intellectual occupation, the Prater, the Glacis, the coffee houses, the Leopoldstadt Theater are the only objects of their thoughts and desires. These they must attain, and if they cannot accomplish this by honorable means, they enlist among the ten thousand *Naderers,* from whom they receive their weekly ducat.

A *Wiener Frucht,* a Vienna sprig, goes even in Austria for the *ne plus ultra* of frivolity, thoughtlessness, and sensuality. Proud as a Frenchman is to have been brought up in Paris or to be thought a Parisian, the Hungarian, Bohemian, Pole, or Italian would be little flattered to be taken for a Viennese. But let us be just: what they are, they have been made by their masters; what is left them, is entirely their own — a kind heart, an unbounded hospitality, and an obsequiousness which seems to bespeak the consciousness of their own inferiority and degradation. The Viennese thinks himself infinitely honored if you drink his wine or eat his dinner. "*Belieben Euer Graden unsern Sitz einzunehmen*" — Please your grace to take our seat?" said a well-dressed gentleman with his lady, who occupied one of the locked seats in the pit and heard us conversing in the English language; and when told that we had just come from our box, he asked whether we would not confer the favor on him to dine at his house, as he was very fond of hearing English spoken. Though you will never hear good sense or a serious word, yet these people show themselves as they are, without the least ostentation or pride. Their faults are those of thoroughly spoiled children, kept in ignorance of their rights by a demoralizing guardian who wishes to prolong his tutorship.

Vienna, considered as a city, is neither the vast London nor the beautiful Paris. It is neither the elegant Berlin nor the gorgeous St. Petersburg. It is the massive headquarters of a massive Government and of a naturally powerful oligarchy. In nobleness it is inferior to Venice; to Milan in beauty; to Prague in picturesque effect; and to Buda in its situation. What Vienna is, it has become gradually, almost without the assisting hand of the Government; if we except the present Emperor, who indeed seems to have intended to give his capital a more uniform aspect. But, except his happy idea of buying and pulling down the shops which surrounded the Cathedral, his other embellishments, the Technological Institution, the New Bank and Gate bear the same tame character which is visible throughout. A refined taste with a little vigor into the bargain might have given to Vienna quite another character and secured the legs and limbs of the curious foreigner; who, if he be doomed here to walking, may learn better than anywhere else to mind his legs. This, however, would interfere with ancient rights; and though the Austrian Government is not overly scrupulous in the use of the scalping knife in matters more vital, yet these things remain as they are.

Of the hundred-and-ten streets which cross Vienna in a circumference of three miles,(N-22) most of them are narrow, all of them crooked, but they are well-paved and lined with massive palaces and palace-like houses, the huge dimensions of which bid defiance to everything of a similar nature.

There is the house of Count Starhemberg, a present of the Emperor to this family for the gallant defense of Vienna against the Turks, inhabited by more than 2000 people. The palaces of the Archduke Charles, the Princes Liechtenstein, Lobkowitz, Schwarzenberg, Esterházy, etc. yield to it in the number of their inhabitants, but not in size. On every bypath, on every corner, your eye is struck with some huge palace of a nobleman. As the houses of the citizens correspond exactly in height with those of the nobility, they present, on the whole, an immense and imposing mass of stately and colossal buildings, interrupted here and there by moderate apertures which they call squares: of these the Joseph's Place is the noblest, and the Graben the gayest. Wherever you happen to be, the spire of St. Stephen is your guide and regulates your wanderings through the intricate mazes. It was, with its church, begun in the year 1171, one of the grandest monuments of Gothic architecture; visibly, however, influenced by the Moorish taste which prevailed at this time. The Strasbourg Minster is more airy; the Milan Cathedral nobler and more splendid; but the Viennese is the more awfully grand. The eye gazes with astonishment at these gigantic arches, springing up to such an enormous height; yet all in the interior is dark and somber. The light which dimly shines through the painted-glass windows is hardly sufficient to distinguish objects. It is a true representation of the character of the Dark Age in which this temple sprang up; when God and his world were enveloped in darkness and only known through the painted medium of the Roman Pontiff and his suite. On the outside of the doors indulgences were affixed, promising to the credulous attendants at divine service, at Maria Stiegen, an indulgence of forty days.

Though this church holds the first rank among the fourteen capital churches which, together with forty smaller ones, receive the pious; yet that of the Augustine monks is the Aulic church. It contains the embalmed hearts of the Emperors and the mausoleum of the Archduchess Christina, sufficiently known not to need any farther description. A grand mass heard in this church, the music of which is the most celebrated in Vienna, is, more than anything else, adapted to give an idea of Catholicism and Catholic worship. Before the altar are the priest and his assistants, dressed in gaudy robes, with a number of priestlings, incensing, bowing, and dancing attendance with an alertness which shows anything but piety, and contrasts strangely with the simplicity and dignity of our Protestant worship. Four or five bells are incessantly ringing from the side altars, where other priests hurry over their masses, surrounded by standing and kneeling devotees who perform their Sunday duty of hearing a mass. The priest who is able to do it in the shortest time, about twelve minutes, is surrounded by the greatest crowd. In the pews, which run up on both sides of the aisles, the fashionable world is seated; and in the open space of the nave are the dandies of Vienna, walking to and fro, ogling, holding conversations, not only with their eyes, but even *viva voce*. There is a bustle, a running, a crossing, a noise which excites anything but serious reflection and is only overpowered by the powerful notes of the organ and the score of instruments which pour forth their delicious sounds. As soon as the concert, either vocal or instrumental, is over, the whole crowd hastens to the doors, leaving priest, divine service, everything to do its business unmolested and alone. Before the mass is half-finished, the church has lost two-thirds of its inmates. Still fewer attend the sermon; not more than twenty-five persons of the thousands who, an hour before, crowded the church. Can we wonder any longer that the Catholic Church produces more infidels than the Protestant creed?

A concert in the Argyll Rooms or even at Covent Garden is far more calculated to excite a serious thought than this mock service. But it is fair to state that this is only the case with a few of the privileged churches, as they are called, selected by the fashionables for their rendezvous. But among these at the church of the Augustine monks and at St. Michael's church you will seldom meet a nobleman of high standing, unless he be of the Prime Minister's school. The rest of the churches are attended by a steadier class, and for better purposes. The garrisons march in battalions to their respective churches, hear mass and a sermon, and return again in a body. The civil officers are equally anxious to perform their Christian duty; and the lower classes are crowding into the church of Maria Stiegen to hear Father Werner and Co.'s sermons. The hundreds of bells which are ringing from six till twelve o'clock, with the glittering equipages rolling in every direction, are the only sounds to be heard on a Sunday morning. The good people of Vienna, however, make amends for this loss of time after dinner: from three o'clock till eleven the city is literally in a musical and sensual uproar. Wherever you go, the sound of musical instruments will reach your ears. Whatever family of the middle class you enter, the pianoforte is the first object which strikes your eyes; you are hardly seated, and a flagon filled with wine, another with water, and Pressburg biscuits placed before you, when the host will tell Caroline to play a tune to the gentleman. To play is their pride, and in that consists chiefly the education of the middle classes. Children begin in their fourth and fifth year, and are pretty proficient in their sixth. A new opera of Rossini in the Kärntnertor Theater will, with these good people, produce quite as much and even more excitement than the opening of the Parliament in London. Their opera is, however, splendid, and Mozart's *Zauberflöte* (magic flute) or *Don Juan*, heard in the Kärntnertor Theater, is a delicious enjoyment. The ballets in the same are inferior to the Parisian. How little propensity the Viennese have even to serious music, Haydn's *Creation*, performed in the Imperial Riding School by 350 musicians, sufficiently proved. Though the grandest performance I ever witnessed, yet it was but thinly attended. Nothing, however, is more striking than the numerical order and regularity visible even in the midst of this chaos of sensuality. Hardly has the clock sounded eleven than city and suburbs, as with a magic stroke, are hushed into deep silence. Everybody is, or should be, at home: and crying, singing, or the least noise in the streets are things unheard of. Everyone must here keep good hours. Vienna is indeed a city of contrasts; here you may find the most abject dissoluteness and undeviating steadiness, a high degree of learning and the grossest ignorance, the most contemptible servility and a noble independent spirit.

Austria, and in particular Vienna, possesses some excellent institutions. Its Code of civil, criminal, and ecclesiastical (the canon) laws, is the best on the continent and superior by far to the Code Napoleon. Austria is indebted for it to its Joseph, who, after the manumission of the peasantry and of his subjects from the shackles of the Roman See, new-modeled the laws of Maria Theresa and of his ancestors. He instituted a commission for this purpose, selected from the members of the Supreme Tribunal of Justice, Hofgesetzgebungs Commission, and the professors of the juridical faculty. This code is continued to the present time and now bears the name of the Codex of Francis I. The chief ornament of this commission was the Aulic Counselor, Chevalier de Sonnenfels, a man whose juridical works deserve to be known better than those of any practical lawyer living. The faculty of law is still respectable, though its members are said to be inferior to those of Prague in learning. But, of course, the recent system of oppression is equally applied to it.

"You cannot conceive," said the doctor of law and public professor of ——— to me, "what a sad thing it is to speak upon rights, where no rights exist. But I have children, one of whom is in the Imperial service. What is to be done?"

The medical faculty owes its present distinguished standing to the same excellent, but so often misunderstood monarch. This institution has a foundation superior to those of Paris and Berlin. Its medical members may, at least, be said to rival those of the abovementioned capitals. Its anatomical theater and collection of preparations deserve admiration. It is frequently resorted to by foreigners who, indeed, can nowhere have a better opportunity of proficiency than here. The Clinical Institution is excellent. The botanical, mineralogical and zoological treasures, deposited in twenty-five salons, are immense. They contain nearly specimens of the whole earth.

The Oriental Academy, under the direction of the Aulic counselor Hammer, enjoys the particular attention of the Emperor: it has certainly done wonders, and to it in part may be attributed the intimacy of the Court of Austria with the Ottoman Porte. There are, besides, a number of other public and excellent institutions; as the Technological School, that of the *Bombardier, Ingenieur,* and Artillery

School, under the direction of the well-known Colonel Augustin. But though there is no want of men of profound learning, they are really separated, not only from the people, but even from each other. An *ingenieur* in Vienna is nothing else but an *ingenieur*, as such he knows perfectly well his science, but nothing more. A professor of the civil law will have his codex fully in his power, but to financial or political matters he is an utter stranger. Unless you touch on his particular branch, you are inclined to think him an absolute ignoramus. They are complete machines through which the Government carries its measures into execution.(N-23)

This would be impossible in any other country besides Austria, where, notwithstanding the great means of public information, public light is so confined. The only public newspaper which deserves this appellation is the *Austrian Observer*, whose editor is Pilat, private secretary to Prince Metternich. But though the rest of the public newspapers for Vienna and the whole Empire amount to no more than twenty-five, and never contain political or financial statements and discussions, yet they are conducted throughout by public officers, and are under the immediate control of no less personages than the governors or vice-kings of the provinces and kingdoms. The same is the case with literary journals. Foreign journals are not entirely prohibited, yet they, as well as their readers, are watched with a prying vigilance. This and their high prices may account for the political darkness in which these poor *savans* are involved, and which sometimes produces strange mistakes in these deep studied men.

It has been made a reproach that this Empire has produced so few men of literary talents. Austria is an accumulation of kingdoms and provinces, with different languages, manners, and customs. Bohemia had its writers when under its own kings, but they are now literally chained down. In Hungary there are three languages spoken and written: the Latin, as the language of the Government, of the Diet, and of the Tribunals of Justice; the Hungarian, the language of the people; and the German. It would be difficult to write in any of those tongues and to find a sufficient reading public.

Austria itself, the smallest part of the Empire, was scarcely unfettered by Joseph II when a host of writers sprang up; most of them poor enough, but some of eminence. Alxinger, Heinrich and Matthias Collin, rank high as poets. *Regulus* and *Balboa* are inferior to

Schiller's and Goethe's tragedies, but to none else. Even at present, the Burg Theater possesses one of the brightest new stars of Germany in its poet, the Viennese Grillparzer, an amiable young man who entered the list of dramatic authors with a terrific and fatal piece, *Schicksalsstück,* or, as it is called, an imitation of Müllner's *Schuld,* and Werner's *Twenty-eighth February.* He soon after founded his reputation on one of the most delicate tragedies which Germany possesses — the *Sappho.* It ranks immediately after Goethe's *Iphigenia in Tauris.* The author has, notwithstanding his strict adherence to the unities of Aristotle, succeeded in diffusing throughout his piece a glow, a melancholy softness, and a freshness which breathe of Grecian air; certainly not an easy matter with so hackneyed a topic as Sappho and with only three persons in the drama. Mrs. Schroeder, as *Sappho,* does ample justice to this beautiful poem.

Grillparzer held, when he produced his *Sappho,* a petty court office in one of the Aulic tribunals, worth £50 a year. The universal sensation, which this *chef-d'œuvre* excited, induced his friends to recommend him to his Majesty for preferment to an office (*Hof concipist*), producing £120 sterling. "Let me alone with your hot-brained Grillparzer," said the Emperor sullenly; "He would make verses instead of reports!"

Neglected and harassed, the poor fellow accepted, after his return from Italy, the appointment of poet of the Imperial Burg Theater with a salary of 2000 florins (£200 sterling); a sum sufficient in Vienna for a single gentleman to live upon in a rather fashionable style. His subsequent production did not answer the just expectations entertained from his Muse. His *Medea* is a long-winded, tame heroine, visibly influenced by fear and the trammels of the Austrian censorship.

A more fettered being than an Austrian author surely never existed. A writer in Austria must not offend against any Government; nor against any minister; nor against any hierarchy, if its members be influential; nor against the aristocracy. He must not be liberal — nor philosophical — nor humorous — in short, he must be nothing at all. Under the catalogue of offenses are comprehended not only satires and witticisms; — nay, he must not explain things at all, because they might lead to serious thoughts. If he ventures to say anything upon these subjects, it must be done in that devout and reverential tone which befits an Austrian subject, who presumes to lift the veil from these *ticklish secrets!* What would have become of Shakespeare had he been doomed to live or to write in Austria? Should an Austrian author dare to write contrary to the views of the Government, his writings would be not only mutilated, but he himself regarded as a contagious person with whom no faithful subject should have any intercourse. Should he, however, go so far as to publish his work out of the Empire — in Germany; a thing almost impossible, owing to the omnipotence of Austria there; — this attempt would be considered and punished as little short of high treason. Compared to the fetters under which the Austrian *literati* groan, their brethren of the quill in Germany are absolute autocrats.

There is in Vienna a nobleman of considerable talent who, with a zeal seldom to be met with, rummaged all the old castles and dusty parchments of the Austrian nobility. He fell into disgrace for writing one of the most harmless productions which, however, did not coincide exactly with the views of the Government. All his own and his uncle's endeavors in the Tyrol could not appease Imperial suspicions; and he remains stained with the greatest crime in Austria — liberalism! — though he has since produced a number of historical essays and a Plutarch in which he proves that all the Austrian monarchs were models of heroism and virtue, even Albert I and Ferdinand II not excepted!!

Who would, under these and similar circumstances, dare to draw upon himself the animadversion of a monarch who thinks and asserts that philosophy, poetry, and history are dangerous things, only fit to turn the heads of the youths and to fill them with good-for-nothing nonsense?

When his Majesty visited Bohemia and Prague the last time, *Hans Klachel of Prelautsch* (the Abdera of Bohemia) was performed; when he attended the sittings of the Diet in Buda, *The Burghers of Vienna*. According to these broad hints and the still broader expressions, these things, as he calls them, are treated. The Burg Theater is literally a thorn in his eyes; it is fettered in every way. Goethe, Schiller, Müllner, and Houwald are not only woefully mangled, but the person is even carefully watched who shows a predilection for *Wallenstein* or *William Tell*. The ballets and operas of the Kärtnertor Theater are, on the contrary, highly patronized, but, above all, the Leopoldstadt or Casperl Theater, as the Viennese call it. Its hero is a Mr. Schuster, whose exterior — he is an ugly hunchback — raises shouts of laughter before he even opens his mouth. Its poet is a Mr. Bäuerle who furnishes regularly every month a new piece. As these farces are innocent in the Austrian sense of the word — viz. contain only obscenities — they pass the censor unmolested.

I saw Schuster in the abovementioned *Burghers of Vienna*, a farce from the period of the French wars, when the citizens had to mount the guard. Honest Schuster is on duty, pacing impatiently up and down, laying his gun now on his right, again on his left shoulder, looking at his watch, when several of his fellow-burghers drop in. Of course it is impossible for him to resist the temptation. To complete his comfort, his paramour arrives, loaded with every species of provision. While he enjoys his bottle of Bisamberg in the next tavern, his officer unexpectedly visits the guard. The search after the deserter, the intercession of the damsel, who takes the officer aside and offers him several things of whose import she gives an idea by kissing him, form the plot and incidents of this and similar pieces. While the income of all the other theaters is deficient through the crippling hand of the censor, that of the Leopoldstadt yields a yearly surplus of more than £5000, a great sum in Austria. The manner in which every channel and medium of public information is either stopped or diverted, according to the views of the Government, baffles every description. There is not a city in the world with more museums, galleries, collections, or libraries — but they are dead treasures. A tour through the salons of the university and its library is painful to one's ears and eyes. The library is one of the richest in Europe in medical, juridical, historical, and philosophical works, but chains are bound round its best contents. The same is the case with the Imperial Library, containing an immense salon of 240 by 546 feet.

It is true, that to all these scientific institutions and collections, both public and private, a foreigner has not only free access (except to the prohibited books), but these good people are delighted if they have an opportunity of showing what they possess. When we visited the palace of the Archduke Charles (formerly the Prince of Saxe Teschen), our progress through the splendid but somewhat whimsically furnished apartments was arrested by his Imperial

Highness, who was in the next room. As soon as the Archduke understood that foreigners were there, he retired into another room, and we had ample leisure to examine the Ivory and Ebony Rooms, as they are called, with the rest of the gorgeous apartments.

But a proper sense and use of these valuable treasures, a love of arts and sciences, a respect for distinguished talents you would in vain seek for in Vienna. The former are kept as a sort of furniture, as a show to look upon, and little else. Even distinguished writers, as G———tz or S———l, are here paid, not so much to write as not to write; and they are considered as intellectual or literary tradesmen. In the Belvedere, the palace of Prince Liechtenstein, or the gallery of Count Lamberg you will perhaps meet a straggling gentleman occasionally sitting down in a corner and making a copy of a Christ or a Madonna, but that is all.

The tide runs in Vienna towards gross sensuality in the people — mute obedience in the public officers; — gloom or dissoluteness among the high nobility, and towards the most complete despotism in the Government, which grasps with the iron claws of its emblem — the double eagle — the whole Empire and keeps it in its baneful embraces.

NOTES

Note 1. *p.* 11.

Among the literary curiosities there is a recently published work, proposing, as a deserving monument for the commemoration of the regained liberty of Europe from Napoleon's despotism, the excavation of our globe as far as to the Antipodes.

The treasures which the author is sure would be found in the interior of the earth, about 1000 miles from the surface, would, in his opinion, amply repay the first expenses. With the earth, rocks, the treasures of gold and silver, he desires the sovereigns of Europe, whom he invites to the execution of his great scheme, to build cities, erect mountains, etc.

Note 2. *p.* 11.

It is almost superfluous to observe that the ambassadors of this German Diet are mere censors watching the German literature, and that they have not the least legislative, judicial, or executive power.

Note 3. *p.* 11.

When I passed through Heidelberg, the unfortunate ex-king of Sweden (Count Gustafsson) alighted in the same hotel where I stopped. He had just left the stagecoach and entered the dining room of the *Posthof*, his portmanteau under his arm, dressed plain and rather poorly, and without a servant. The room was crowded with passengers and students; the conversation, though not noisy, yet lively. As soon as the ex-monarch entered, a deep respectful silence ensued, the students left off smoking, and the gentleman who occupied the head of the table rose to make place for the distinguished guest. The landlord approached him and asked whether he would not be pleased to hear the band of musicians which just entered. He consented, but they were not permitted to address him for the petty customary compliment, as it was generally known that he was very poor and reduced to the necessity of pawning at Basel his portmanteau. There was not a sneer, not the least contempt shown towards the dethroned monarch, so reduced in his pecuniary means. A deep respect was legible on the countenances of the whole company, as far from servile cringing to highlife, as low contempt of fallen greatness. I could not help expressing my satisfaction to one of the students, a beautiful, noble, and proud-looking young fellow, dressed in the Teutonic costume. "Sir," said he, seriously, "we would not show so much respect towards the Emperor of Austria, but Count Gustafsson is unfortunate," and raising his voice emphatically, "Woe to the wretch who adds to the load of the oppressed!"

Note 4. p. 12.

When in Teplitz, I took an excursion with some Polish ladies and gentlemen. Our conversation turned on Poniatowski: "Oh," said the beautiful S——, "you should indeed have seen him when he drove his phaeton and eight wild steeds, standing and alone, through Warsaw's royal streets." All the ladies were in tears, and the gentlemen pretty near to it.

Note 5. p. 29.

The Russians, Poles, Bohemians, and Wends are tribes of the extensive nation of the Slaven, or Slavs, as they call themselves.

Note 6. p. 30.

During the reign of Ferdinand II of infatuated memory, there were in the kingdom of Bohemia not less than 50,000 printed books and manuscripts in the Bohemian tongue burnt by the Jesuits.

Note 7. p. 39.

This kind-hearted soul received soon after an invitation from Frederick the Great, with an offer of 5000 florins salary; his own was but 800 florins, £80. While hesitating, he was called before his Sovereign, Joseph II, who addressed him; "Mozart, you are going to leave me." Overpowered by the kind tone in which these words were pronounced, he, sobbing and tears gushing from his eyes, could only reply, "No, never will I leave your Majesty!"

Note 8. p. 40.

The furnaces of Genitz, Horshowitz, and Purglitz, constructed of freestone with iron roofs, are said to be superior to everything of their kind on the continent. I have not seen them.

Note 9. p. 40.

In the reign of Ferdinand II there were in Prague two universities, the one founded by Charles IV, the other by the Calixtines (Hussites). The latter was abolished by Ferdinand. Though the ancient Bohemian writers concur in the statement, that in the time of Huss, 30,000 students were in Prague, yet this is surely a mistake. Even in the present times the whole body of students at all the European universities scarcely amounts to this number.

Note 10. p. 42.

The elementary schools in the Austrian Empire are equally regulated by the Government and in each province superintended by a *Scholasticus*, a Canon of the Chapter, who receives the reports of his inferior officer and is under the control of the Government. Private schools are prohibited. It must be allowed that the system of education, though not on a liberal, is certainly established on an extensive plan. There is not a village without its elementary school;

the teachers are either paid by the Government or by the proprietor of the domain. The children of the poor are educated *gratis*. The professors of Latin schools, lycæums, (colleges) and universities are entirely independent of the students and receive their salary from the crown, from £80 to £200 a year. Extraordinary lectures are seldom permitted, and, if held, the stipends (4*s*. for half-a-year) are so trifling that most of the professors seldom resort to this means of bettering their circumstances. The stipend which students have to pay to the Government for their instruction is in universities 2*s*. a month; but almost all of them are exempt from paying even this trifle, and it requires only a petition to the Government to make them exempt.

Note 11. *p*. 73.

Tokay wine is without doubt the best wine in the world. With its taste, spirit, and fire nothing can be compared: it is among the wines, what the pineapple is among the fruits. The reason why this wine is less properly valued in foreign countries, Russia and Poland excepted, is that there are four sorts of it. The first, called Essence, is even in Tokay or Vienna sold at not less than £2 sterling a bottle; so in proportion, the lesser sorts. What is drunk in London and Paris as Tokay, is genuine English or French produce.

Note 12. *p*. 78.

It is universally asserted in well-informed circles that Metternich received from the R——n C——t a salary superior to that which he enjoyed from the Austrian Emperor; and that the latter knew of this circumstance. Whether this be true or not we do not know, and never took the pains of ascertaining it. The following authenticated circumstance is, however, very singular. A person who had demands to a large amount on the Austrian treasury for provisions delivered to the army and was unable to obtain payment, applied to the Emperor. "Have you been to Counselor N——?" demanded the Emperor. "Yes, your Majesty." "What does he say?" " I must wait." "Well, go again; but if you will drive your coach," rubbing at the same time his thumb and forefinger, "you must smear the wheels!"

Note 13. p. 78.

Abhorring, as we do, the Austrian despotism, yet from these very probable results, along with the natural power and influence of its aristocracy — this monarchy cannot continue a despotic one; and if it does, the links of the empire will give way.

Note 14. p. 84.

While he sends the apparently liberal but wily E——y to L——n, the Apostolic A——y directs the councils of the French aristocracy and clergy in P——s. In F——t, where the censorship of Germany is established, the *bel esprit* Mr. de B——n must do with no other business and knowledge than that of reading and watching German novels and pamphlets. The lofty and high spirited A——t of R——a is entrusted to the scarcely less lofty, but pliable P——e H——a.

"You would be astonished," said H. "at the noblemen of high character among the different aristocracies who are in the interest of this man, in every country and in every town."

Note 15. p. 84.

The Habsburg family is, for the acquisition and present quiet possession of Hungary, principally indebted to the family of Esterházy. In the year 1805, after the fatal capture of the Austrian army at Ulm, the Austrian forces on the Danube were under the command of Prince A——y, who was entrusted with the breaking of the wooden bridge leading across the Danube at Vienna. He disobeyed his instructions, and Napoleon marched without obstacle in pursuit of the Austrian and Russian armies in Moravia. The loss of the battle at Austerlitz was the consequence. Archduke Charles with the Austrian army was scarcely two days' march from the field of battle — but he came too late. The outcry of treachery against A——y was universal; in Great Britain, France, Prussia, or Russia he would undoubtedly have been shot. In Austria he came off with a few years' banishment from the Imperial headquarters, Vienna.

Note 16. p. 85.

Among other curiosities, there is in the Milan library the diploma of nobility conferred by the Duke Galeazzo on the family of his mistress. The reason of this elevation is candidly enough expressed in the diploma: *"Ob delectationem præcipuam corpori nostro ab illa præstitam, etc."*

Pope Sixtus V raised his sister, a washerwoman, to the rank of Princess. The next day Pasquino appeared in a dirty shirt. "Why this?" he is asked. "Don't you know my washerwoman has become a Princess?" was the cutting answer. The Pope was so incensed that he promised one thousand crowns to the person who would detect the author: none appeared. He repeated his offer with the promise that no bodily harm should be done if the author offered himself. This stratagem succeeded. The author claimed the thousand crowns; they were given to him — his life spared, but his tongue cut out.

How a number of the first French families descend from the Valières, Gabrielles, etc. is known: we think it, however, necessary to observe that in speaking of the respectability of the Austrian aristocracy, we limit this term strictly to the national Hungarian, Bohemian, and even Austrian noblemen: not, however, those who made their fortune in Austria and came from Italy, Germany, or France. There are a great number of such families; though many of them are respectable, they are the chief cause of the outcry which is so unjustly raised against the dissoluteness of the Austrian nobility by less discerning people. A national nobility is everywhere respectable; and it requires certainly a high degree of evil propensity to deviate entirely from noble ancestors and to fix the stigma of infamy before the eyes of a native country on one's self: a transplanted nobleman, however, is scarcely good for anything.

Note 17. p. 87.

The Austrian Infantry consists of thirty battalions of grenadiers, each 800 men strong; of sixty-four regiments of infantry, and seventeen regiments of Banat infantry, each regiment of three battalions in time of peace 800 men strong, in time of war six battalions, each 1000 men. To this body is added in time of war the Landwehr militia which serve as regular soldiery, 120,000 men strong, and the Hungarian Insurrections Army, 50,000 men. To these come eight battalions of riflemen (Jäger), five regiments of artillery, 20,000 men with a corresponding train of bombardiers. The cavalry consists of twelve regiments of hussars, 800 men strong; eight regiments of cuirassiers, eight of dragoons, four regiments of lancers, each 800 men strong. The whole army amounts in time of peace to 270,000 men, in time of war to 650,000. These troops are recruited from the German, Polish, and Italian dominions, according to the law of conscription from which, however, Hungary is exempt, in conformity to its constitution. Private soldiers are still subject to flogging and to the guntlope. The pay of a common soldier of the infantry is six kreutzer, 2*d.* from which he has to pay for his half-pound of meat; with the rest he is provided. The grenadiers, *artillerists*, and *cavallerists* have eight and ten kreutzers, from 2 1/2*d.* to 3*d.* The monthly pay of the officers is, for an ensign, £2 2*s.*; for a lieutenant, £2 8*s*; for a premier-lieutenant, £2 18*s.;* for a second-captain, £3 12*s.*; for a captain (Hauptmann), £7 8*s.*; a major has £120 a year; a colonel-lieutenant, £180; a colonel, £350; a field marshal £1600 The officers of the staff, from the major upwards, have horse rations: the major 3, colonel-lieutenants 4, colonels 6, major-generals 8, field marshals 16.

The colonels have the jus gladii. — The regiments are in each province under the command of a General Commandant who make their reports to the Council of War, Hofkriegsrat, the supreme and central tribunal of the whole army.

Note 18. *p.* 88.

There will scarcely be an Austrian nobleman who does not read and write the English, French, and Italian languages perfectly well. Most of them keep the newspapers of these countries: in this point they are, of course, exempt from the general prohibition with respect to gazettes.

Note 19. *p.* 89.

There are chief journals: the *Sammler*, the *Annals of the Austrian Empire*; the *Annals of Literature*, and one or two journals of inferior note.

Each province, which has a Government of its own, is allowed one newspaper.

Note 20. *p.* 93.

The Germans distinguish in their waltzes: — the first, the Landser (country dance), is a slow waltz; the second, the waltz keeps the middle between the Landser and Den Deutschen, which latter they dance very quick.

Note 21. *p.* 97.

There are in Vienna the following tribunals: — The Council of the State, headed by the Emperor as president and Prince Metternich as vice president. The Ministry of the Interior, or Chancelleries for Bohemia, Austria, Italy, Poland, with two Counselors of the State and fifty Aulic counselors, each of whom has his own department of business.

The Chancelleries for Hungary and Transylvania, with two Counselors of the State and thirty-five Aulic counselors.

The Ministry of Justice, with two Counselors and sixteen Counselors of the Court.

Ministry of Foreign Affairs, with two Counselors of State and ten Aulic counselors.

Ministry of Treasury (Hofkammer), with two State Counselors and seventy-five Aulic counselors.

Ministry of War (Hofkriegsrat), with twenty-five Aulic counselors.

President of the Police, with three Aulic counselors. According to the old city regulations, the second and third floors of the houses of citizens in the city proper are exclusively to be let to officers. There is in the Austrian cities and towns a distinction made between the houses of citizens and those of the nobility, when registered in the Landtafel (the record office of the nobility). The latter pay less taxes, are exempt from the quartering of the soldiers, but cannot carry on trade. The former are registered in the records of the city.

Note 22. *p.* 101.

Vienna with its suburbs is 15 miles in circumference. In Vienna there are one Serbian; one Latin, (for Hungary), and one Hungarian newspaper, besides the *Court Gazette* and the *Austrian Observer*.

Note 23. *p.* 105.

By an Imperial decree, dated 1808, the chair of Religious Philosophy was erected and attached to the philosophical studies. The most erudite men were selected to fill this chair; its effects were astonishing. An intellectual progress was felt throughout, far above what can be imagined. The Austrian academic youth became through these lectures, in fact, Protestants in mind, though professors of Catholicism. "I will," said his Majesty in a cabinet, writing to his Minister of the Interior, Count Saurau, "that my youth shall believe and not dispute the Articles of Faith." Accordingly, everyone had to regulate himself. Those who did not comply immediately with the new command were dismissed from their chairs or imprisoned. The students who revolted were sent to the Turkish frontiers as private soldiers. Among the former was the doctor and professor of this philosophical chair in Vienna. His place was filled by a monk of the newly-instituted Order of the Licorians, a Mr. Madelener. The outcry against these and similar journeymen of the Roman See was universal. Lampoons, everything was tried; even the Emperor's own brother, the Archduke Rudolf, Cardinal Archbishop of Olmütz, begged to be excused from receiving them into his see; but the Emperor wanted pious men, and accordingly they obtained the Church of Maria, with a capital of £20,000 sterling, for their support.

Nearly from the same motives and views there has been (1821) a Protestant Theological Institution established; to prevent Austrian Protestant subjects from visiting German universities. Its director, a Mr. Glatz, is an excellent preacher and scholar; the institution, however, is a very meager substitute for a Protestant theological faculty.

THE END

GLOSSARY

For several of the following clarifications I am indebted to the scholarship of Eduard Castle in *Der große Unbekannte: Das Leben von Charles Sealsfield (Carl Postl)* (Wien: Manutius Presse, 1952), Victor Klarwill in *Charles Sealsfield, Sämtliche Werke*, Bd. 3, Karl J.R. Arndt, Hrsg. (Hildesheim: Olms Presse, 1972), and of Primus-Heinz Kucher in his edition of *Austria As It Is* (Wien: Böhlau Verlag, 1994).

ad hominem = an argument appealing to emotion rather than reason, a personal attack rather than a reasoned response

Albion = England

Alxinger, Henry and Matthias Collin . . . Regulus, Balboa = the Austrian dramatists Johann Baptist Edler von Alxinger (1755-1797); Heinrich Collin (1772-1811), the author of the tragedies *Regulus* and *Balboa*; and his younger brother Matthäus Casimir von Collin (1779-1824)

Andreas Hofer = (1767-1810), Austrian patriot and freedom fighter, resisted foreign rule of the Tyrol, was eventually court-martialed and shot by the French

Antipodes = diametrically opposed parts of the earth; here: from the North to the South Pole

aqua tofana = poison, a liquid containing arsenic

Archduke Charles = Karl Ludwig Johann Josef, Archduke of Austria (1771-1847)

Archduke Rudolf, Cardinal Archbishop of Olmütz = brother of Emperor Francis

Argyll Rooms . . . Covent Garden = the Argyll Rooms, on Regent Street, were the first home of the Philharmonic Society of London in 1813; Covent Garden, a square, formerly a convent garden; adjacent to the former market site stands the Royal Opera House, now known as Covent Garden

arrondissement = an administrative district in some French cities; also a play on words, here meaning both a region or locale, but also the "rounding off" or reacquisition of lost territories

A——r's presence = Alexander I, Czar of Russia, present at the Congress of Vienna

Augarten . . . Prater . . . Glacis = public parks in Vienna: the Augarten or meadow gardens directly opposite the Old City, across the Danube; the Prater, a former hunting preserve on meadowland bordering the Danube, also across the river, has been open to the public since 1766; the Glacis, the gentle slope running down from the Hofburg outside the old city wall (today, the Burgring)

Aulic = pertaining to Imperial offices under the Austrian Habsburgs

A——t of R——a = probably Autocrat of Russia, meaning Alexander

auto da fe = in broad terms, the burning of a heretic

Banat = region comprised of much of modern-day Hungary, Rumania, Yugoslavia—in contrast to more civilized areas, to be sent there was considered a form of punishment or unofficial banishment

banks = benches

Baron K——a = Baron Johann von Kutschera, Field Marshall-Lieutenant and aide-de-camp to the Emperor

Baron *Kleyle* = though the original text has "Baron Kuorn," most think this a misspelling for Baron Franz Joachim Ritter von Kleyle

Baron *Stein* = Heinrich Friedrich Karl von und zum Stein (1757-1831), Prussian statesman whose reforms turned Prussia into a modern state

B—— C—— = Carl Breindl

beadles = minor officials who preserve order at civic functions

bel esprit = a man of wit, a brilliant mind

Bella gerant alii, tu, felix Austria, nube = Let others wage wars: you, fortunate Austria, marry

Berthier = Napoleon's aide, Louis Alexandre Berthier (1753-1815), Marshal of France

Bolzano = professor of philosophy Bernhard Bolzano (1781-1848), accused of promoting liberal ideas within the Theological Faculty at Prague, was dismissed and lived in poverty till his death; apparently a great influence on young Postl/Sealsfield

and his quest for freedom and critical thought
B——n D—— = according to the anecdote, Baron Johann von Kutschera, Field Marshall-Lieutenant and aide-de-camp to the Emperor
B——n V——n = possibly General Baron von Vincent, Austrian chargé d'affaires in Paris
Böttiger and Nostiz = the Weimar journalist and critic Karl August Böttiger (1760-1835), and the romantic writer Gottlob Adolf Ernst von Nostiz (1765-1836) who wrote under the pen name of Arthur von Nordstern.
Brother Jonathan = generic name for a New Englander, thus for Americans and America in general.
Brutus, Cato = Marcus Junius Brutus (85-42 B.C.), one of Caesar's assassins, and Marcus Porcius Cato (95-46 B.C.), Roman statesman whose honesty, incorruptibility, and loyalty to the state were exemplary — thus examples of bad and good citizens were employed to test the future allegiance of young pupils
bucklers = small round shields held at arm's length
Bucks County, Pennsylvania = allusion to a traditionally-German area of southeast Pennsylvania, familiar to Sealsfield, an ostensible "native" of that state
bullion = a gold lace or braid
bumper = a brimming cup or glass
cabotte = great coat
cabriolet = a light, two-wheeled (one-horse) carriage with a folding hood
calash = a four-passenger carriage with a folding top
Caleb, the worthy factotum of Ravenswood = the butler Caleb Balderston, epitome of the faithful servant, from Sir Walter Scott's novel *The Bride of Lammermoor* (1819).
Calixtines (Hussites) = moderate followers of Huss during the Hussite Wars (1420-1433), an attempt to implement religious and political reforms in Bohemia
calpacs = tall black hats of sheepskin or felt
career = at full speed, at a hectic pace
Casperl Theater = a Punch and Judy show, puppet theater
castagnettes = castanets

castellan = one who oversees a castle or a fort

Ceres, Bacchus, and Venus = Roman gods of harvest, wine, and love, thus Sealsfield's allusion to overindulgence, gluttony, and lust

Charles IV = (1685-1740) Holy Roman Emperor and King of Bohemia, father of Maria Theresa

Chatham-Pitt, Sully, Colbert, or Stein = distinguished statesmen William Pitt, Earl of Chatham (1708-1778) of England; Maximilien de Béthune, Duc de Sully (1560-1641) of France; Jean-Baptiste Colbert (1619-1683) of France; and Baron Karl vom und zum Stein (1757-1831) of Prussia

chausee = roadway

Chevalier de Sonnenfels = Joseph von Sonnenfels (1732-1817), legal scholar who played a major role in shaping the reforms of Joseph II

Chevalier Gerstner = Franz Joseph von Gerstner (1756-1823), engineer, physicist, mathematician who collaborated in the development of the Bohemian iron industry

Choco = Jocko, the Brasilian monkey (from the French Joko, ou: le singe du Brésil); despondent in Paris, Frederick William reportedly also spent much time tobogganing down the slides of the Montagnes Russes

chronique scandaleuse = stories of scandal or gossip at court or among the nobility

cicerone = a guide who conducts sightseers

ci-devant = former

circles = administrative districts or counties

civil list = an annual sum for support and maintenance of the monarch's household, usually raised by taxation; quoted here in British pounds (£).

Clary = Karl Josef, Prince von Clary and Aldringen (1777-1831)

Colloredo = Hieronymus Count Colloredo-Mansfeld (1775-1822)

Colonel Augustin = according to scholars, Sealsfield erred here; the actual director of the Artillery School was Colonel Franz Mandl

con amore = tenderly, with love

Congress of Carlsbad = a conference of ministers from the major German states (among them, Austria, Prussia, Bavaria, Saxony), meeting at the spa of Carlsbad in August, 1819. Under the influence of the Austrian foreign minister, Metternich, the repressive and reactionary Carlsbad Decrees were censorious and intended to suppress nationalistic, liberal, or revolutionary ideas

Congress of Rastatt = 1797-1799, among the states of the Holy Roman Empire, to discuss compensation for territories lost to France during the French Revolutionary Wars

Corinth = one of the largest, wealthiest, oldest, and most powerful cities in ancient Greece, destroyed many times by less-enlightened invaders.

Corneilles, Racines, Montesquieus, and Rousseaus = Pierre Corneille (1606-1684) and Jean Racine (1639-1699) were masters of French tragedy, Baron de La Brède et de Montesquieu (1689-1755) of the political essay, and Jean-Jacques Rousseau (1712-1778) of philosophy and literature; these four represent for Sealsfield the golden age of French enlightenment.

coteries = exclusive social groups with a common purpose or interest

cothurnus = a laced boot often worn by Greek and Roman actors in ancient tragedies

Counselor N—— = possibly Philip von Neumann, diplomat in London

Count Marcolini = Camillo Marcolini (1739-1814), director of the Dresden Art Academy

Count Narbonne . . . Caulaincourt = French generals and statesmen Louis de Narbonne-Lara (1755-1813) and Armand Augustin Louis de Caulaincourt (1772-1827)

Count O'Donnel = Joseph Count O'Donnel (1756-1810), head of the Imperial treasury

Count P—— = presumably Count Fidel Pálffy, head of the Hungarian Chancery

Count Saurau = Minister of the Interior Count Franz Joseph Saurau

Count Stadion = Johann Philipp Karl von Stadion-Warthausen (1763-1824), statesman, foreign minister, and diplomat who served the Habsburg empire during the Napoleonic Wars.

Count Thun = Franz Anton Count von Thun-Hohenstein (1786-1873)

Count Wrbna = Count Rudolf Wrbna-Freudenthal (1761-1823)

crescent = a symbol for the Ottoman Turks

C——t F——n = possibly Count Karl Ficquelmont, Ambassador to St. Petersburg

C——t F——s = possibly the property of Count Festetics in Bohemia *cudgel* = a short heavy club

Dannecker = Johann Heinrich von Dannecker (1758-1841), classical German sculptor

divertissement = diversion, entertainment

divine = a clergyman or theologian

douaniers = toll takers, customs agents

Duke of Ormonde = Presumably James Butler, 1st duke of Ormonde (1610-1688)

Duke of Reichstadt = Napoleon Franz Josef Karl von Reichstadt (1811-1832), the son of Napoleon and Marie Louise of Austria

Duke of Wellington = Arthur Wellesley, the Iron Duke (1769-1852), successful British general who drove the French from Spain and, with Blücher, defeated Napoleon at Waterloo

Emperors Matthias and Rudolph = Matthias (1557-1619), King of Bohemia and Hungary, forced his brother Emperor Rudolph II (1552-1612) to accept religious compromise in Austria, Bohemia, Hungary, and Moravia, though their differences precipitated the Thirty Years' War

en bagatelle = treating the matter as unimportant or insignificant

enfilade of rooms = rooms arranged in opposite and parallel rows

equipages = horse-drawn carriages with their retinue of servants

Erzgebirge = Ore Mountains, in northwestern Bohemia

escadron = cavalry troop

eulogium = eulogy, commendation

Euphrates, Tigris, Araks, and Ganges = four great rivers, "cradles" of great civilizations: the Tigris-Euphrates formed the fertile crescent in Biblical times; the Araks river valley, between Turkey and Armenia, has been thought by some to be the site of the legendary Garden of Eden; the Ganges is the great holy river of India

Euere Durchlaucht (Votre Altesse) = Your highness

exhibits = petitions

Fat King = William I (1781-1864), King of Württemberg

Ferdinand II = (1578-1637), King of Bohemia, allied with the Catholic forces during the Counter-Reformation and Thirty Years' War

fiacre = a small hackney coach

flagon = a large pottery vessel, for wine

flambeaux = flaming torches

florins = in Britain, a silver coin worth two shillings

Franzl = nickname for Emperor Francis I (1768-1835), ultimately victorious over Napoleon, host of the Congress of Vienna in 1815 which made Austria the leading power in Europe; his desire for peace and tranquility was enforced by his minister Metternich, often resulting in repressive measures, informants, and censorship. Nevertheless, he was considered a popular sovereign among his people

Frederick = Frederick the Great (1712-1786) built Prussia into the most powerful German state as a result of his wars, reforms, and enlightened administration

Frederick the Palatine = Frederick V, King of Bohemia, the elector palatine, also known as The Winter King, due to his short-lived reign as a protestant alternative to the Roman Catholic Emperor Ferdinand at the outset of the Thirty Years' War

Frederick William the Third = (1770-1840) King of Prussia; Sealsfield implies here that his cowardice led to his defeat by Napoleon in 1806.

fricassées = cut-up meat, stewed in stock, served in a white sauce

Frint = Dr. Jakob Frint (1766-1834), court chaplain, responsible for religious affairs in the Empire, and Emperor Franz's confessor, who manipulated the dismissal of Bernhard Bolzano in 1820

Gallican church = advocates administrative independence from papal control, here referring to France

G——d d——n = probably "God damn!"

General Kleist = Friedrich Heinrich Ferdinand Emil von Kleist (1762-1828) who, with the Russian General Ostermann, defeated Vandamme at the Battle of Kulm and Nollendorf

Goethe, Winkelman, Böttiger = here referring to the "connoisseurship," discriminating sensitivity and good taste of Johann Wolfgang von Goethe (1749-1832), the preeminent German poet and dramatist; of Johann Joachim Winckelmann (1717-1768) who coined the classical ideal of "noble simplicity and serene greatness"; of Karl August Böttiger (1760-1835), influential Weimar journalist and critic

Goethe's Torquato Tasso = classical drama from 1790 on the titular hero's immaturity in the face of political responsibility

gold bullion (as decoration) = a braid or fringe of gold threads *golden siècle* = the 19th century, in the minds of the French nobility, was to be a golden age, a return to prerevolutionary, pre-Napoleonic glory and power

Graben = the main street in Vienna that leads to St. Stephen's cathedral

great Corsican = Napoleon, who was born on the island of Corsica in 1769

Green Vault = an extraordinary display of jewelers' craftsmanship from around the world, today in the Dresden Albertinum

grenadiers, artillerists, and cavallerists = army divisions of infantry, artillery, and cavalry

Grillparzer = Franz Grillparzer (1791-1872), Austrian dramatist and poet, author of *Die Ahnfrau* and *Sappho*, the plays to which Sealsfield alludes

Grossbeeren and Bautzen = Napoleon was victorious at the Battle of Bautzen (May 1813), but his generals Oudinot and Reynier were defeated at the Battle of Grossbeeren in August — thus perhaps Sealsfield means the Battle of Gross-Görschen or Lützen, also a French victory

G——tz or S———l = the distinguished writers Friedrich von Gentz (1764-1832), a political writer and statesman; possibly Friedrich von Schlegel (1772-1829), for many years in Austrian service

guntlope = gauntlet

hackney coach = a carriage for public hire

Hammer = Joseph von Hammer-Purgstall (1774-1856), leading orientalist

Hampden, Zizka = John Hampden, 1594-1643, politician, as a protester of unjust taxation, he precipitated the English Civil War; Jan Ziska v. *Trochnow* (Zizka), 1360-1424, courageous field commander of the rebellious Hussites

Handel...Haydn...Graun = the German-born English composer George Frideric Handel (1685-1759, the Austrian classical composer Franz Joseph Haydn (1732-1809), the German opera and oratorio composer Carl Heinrich Graun (1704-1759)

Hans Klachel of Prelautsch = a farcical figure, *Hanns Klachl*, created by Karl Franz Guolfinger, Ritter von Steinsberg; *"the Abdera of Bohemia"* alludes to Christoph Martin Wieland's 1774 novel, *Die Abderiten*, i.e., idiots

Haydn's Creation = the Austrian composer Franz Joseph Haydn (1732-1809) and his great oratorio of 1798

healths = toasts

Hof concipist = court scribe or draftsman, archivist

hogshead = a large cask or barrel, 63 U.S. gallons

Holy Alliance = between Russia, Austria, and Prussia, to maintain the status quo following the defeat of Napoleon; the Austrian Metternich was one of its principal adherents and most rigorous enforcers

Huss and Hieronymus of Prague = the Bohemian religious reformer and nationalist John Huss (Jan Hus, 1369?-1415)) and his friend Hieronymus (Jerome, 1370?-1416); both were burned by the Church as heretics

hussars . . . cuirassiers . . . dragoons . . . lancers = traditional cavalry divisions: light cavalry . . . mounted soldiers with body armor . . . mounted infantry armed with a type of rifle . . . regiments armed with lances

impromptu = improvised, extemporaneous

incogniti = here, without formal recognition from host or hostess

John Bull = the personification of England

jus gladii = the right of the sword, supreme jurisdiction

K——a = Baron Kutschera

Kecskemet = a commercial center in Hungary

King of Prussia = Friedrich William IV (1770-1840)

kreutzers... groschens = monetary units of the day

Krock = mythical ruler during a golden age in prehistoric Bohemia

Lanenstande = this misprint has baffled scholars, though an intelligent guess would be "Donaustrudel," a dangerous whirlpool in the Danube.

Liguorians = followers of saint Alfonso Maria de´ Liguori (1696-1787) who encouraged religious work among the poor; his followers also had great difficulties with the anticlerical government

little Japan = referring to Japan's isolationist, closed-door policy; the island-nation remained closed to world trade until 1854

Lord Findlater's temple = James, Earl of Findlater and Seafield, a Scottish aristocrat living in north Bohemia, had constructed extensive Romantic gardens and parks, also in Carlsbad

Lorenz = Martin von Lorenz, abbot responsible for religious affairs in the Imperial Council and thus in the entire Empire

Lydia and Ephesus = here, representing a legendary "Golden" Age: the fabulously wealthy kingdom of Lydia (in northwest Turkey) and Ephesus, an ancient Greek city (in western Turkey), a leading seaport also known for its enormous wealth

Mack and A——g = Baron Karl Mack von Leiberich (1752-1828) underestimated the mobility of French troops at Ulm (1805) and suffered a tremendous defeat, as did Michael Friedrich von Melas at Marengo (1800)

Madame Sonntag = Henriette Sonntag (1806-1854), famous singer, began her career at the Prague conservatory

Madonna = among Dresden's many art treasures at the time, the *Sistine Madonna*, painted by Raphael, graced the Zwinger

"Mais, mon Prince, cela offensera" - *"Des fantaisies"* = "But, my Prince, that might cause offense." — "You're dreaming!"

mall tunes = presumably melodies in a minor (*"moll"*) key

manes of Waldstein = Waldstein, or Albrecht Wenzel Eusebius von Wallenstein (1583-1634), Bohemian soldier and statesman, commanding general of the armies of the Holy Roman Emperor Ferdinand II during the Thirty Years' War; his alienation from the Emperor and his political-military conspiracies led to his assassination. The venerated spirit (manes) of the dead soldier are believed to inhabit his room in the Pachelbel House

manumission = release, emancipation from slavery

Marengo and Ulm = Napoleonic victory over the Austrian-Russian armies at Marengo (1800) and the capitulation of Austrian forces at Ulm (1805) due to a blunder by the Austrian General Mack

Maria Theresa, Joseph, or Francis = beloved Austrian emperors Maria Theresa (1717-1780, known for her agrarian and administrative reforms), her son Joseph II (1741-1790, who instituted extensive reforms concerning slavery, religious freedoms, the civil service, etc.), and Francis I (1768-1835, ultimately victorious over Napoleon, host of the Congress of Vienna in 1815, thus raising Austria to the leading power in Europe)

Marobudum = Bohemia, after its king, Maroboduus (ca. 20 A.D.)?

maroquin = Moroccan leather

marshal de danse = an individual selected to organize the dancing

metaliquis = metal coins

Metternich = Klemens Wenzel Nepomuk Lothar, Prince of Metternich-Winneburg-Beilstein (born in Koblenz, Germany in 1773, died in Vienna, 1859), an Austrian statesman, minister of foreign affairs from 1809 to 1848, and a champion of conservatism who helped form the victorious alliance against Napoleon I and restored Austria as a leading European power

Miguelites = Portuguese disciples of Dom Miguel Maria Evarist of Braganza (1802-1866), fanatical opponent of constitutional government

Mozart's Zauberflöte or Don Juan = two of the most famous operas by the Austrian composer Wolfgang Amadeus Mozart (1756-1791), *The Magic Flute* and *Don Giovanni*

Mr. Bäuerle = Adolf Johann Bäuerle (1786-1859), dramatist famous for his farces; also journalist, editor of the *Vienna Theater Newspaper* from 1806 until his death

Mr. Glatz = director of the Protestant Theological Institution

Mr. Madelener = a professor of Philosophy from the newly-instituted Order of the Licorians

Mr. Schuster = Ignaz Schuster (1770-1835), actor, famous as the comic figure "Staberl" in various plays

Mrs. Schroeder as Sappho = the tragedienne Sophie Schroeder (1791-1872), in the title role of this classical play by Grillparzer

Mrs. Siddons = the finest English actress of her day, Sarah Siddons (1755-1831)

Müllers, Fichtes, Herders, Schillers, Goethes = the liberal German philosophers or poets Friedrich Müller ("Maler Müller," 1749-1825), Johann Gottlieb Fichte (1762-1814), Johann Gottfried von Herder (1744-1803), Friedrich von Schiller (1759-1805), Johann Wolfgang von Goethe (1749-1832)

Müllner, Houwald = the writers Amadeus Gottfried Adolf Müllner (1774-1829) and Baron Ernst Christoph von Houwald (1778-1845), acknowledged masters of Romantic tragedies of fate

Müllner's Schuld = his extremely successful tragedy *Die Schuld* of 1816, which was widely imitated (here, by Grillparzer), and then soon forgotten

Munkatsch, Komorn, or Spielberg = state prisons

Musselman . . . Moors = Muslims . . . here African servants
nobleman of considerable talent = the allusion is to Baron Joseph von Hormayr zu Hortenburg (1781-1848), a historian and dramatist who was forced to resign from his official post as Imperial Historian and move to Bavaria
Ob delectationem proecipuam corpori nostro ab illa praestitam = On account of the incredible pleasure she gave to my body . . .
old king = Charles X of France (1757-1830), the reigning French king, then 71 years old, who ruled from 1824 until his death
Ostermann = Alexander Ivanovich Count Ostermann-Tolstoi (1772-1857), Russian general who, with Kleist, defeated Vandamme at the Battle of Kulm and Nollendorf
Ottocar = Ottocar II (1230?-1278), King of Bohemia, rebuffed in his attempt to become Holy Roman Emperor due to his unprecedented power, was forced by rival Rudolf I of Habsburg to forfeit all his lands (almost equivalent to the Austrian Empire of 1815!) with the exception of Bohemia and Moravia; he died in battle, trying to reclaim his possessions
Ottoman Porte = Turkey
Palatine = Archduke Joseph Anton Johann (1776-1847), son of Francis
parquetted floors = patterned wooden flooring
pelisses = long cloaks or coats, lined or trimmed with fur
petit gala days = festivities for a small, select group
petites soirées = small, intimate parties for a select group of guests
phaeton = a light, four-wheeled, horse-drawn carriage
Philip of Macedon = Philip V (238-179 B.C.), King of Macedon, to whom it was reportedly said: "Philip, remember thou art mortal" as a check to his ambition
Pilat = private secretary to Prince Metternich, Josef Anton Edler von Pilat (1782-1865), a diplomat and writer, editor of the *Austrian Observer* for 37 years
pipes = wine cask equal to two hogsheads, or 126 U.S. gallons
polonaise = stately Polish processional dance
Poniatowski = Prince Józef Anton Poniatowski (1763-1813), Polish general who led Napoleon's troops against the Russians at the Battle of Leipzig; when his troops were cut off, he plunged his horse into the river and drowned; thus Poniatowski did,

indeed, drown in the Elster river.
poor d——l = poor devil, meaning the King of Prussia, a victim of Napoleon's machinations
Pope Sixtus V . . . Pasquino = Sixtus V (Felice Peretti, 1521-1590), generally known as one of the great figures of the Catholic Reformation; Pasquino is the stock character in a "Pasquinade," a brief and generally anonymous satirical comment in prose or verse that ridicules a contemporary leader or national event, here the Pope
portmanteau = a large traveling bag
P——p of S——g, a born P——ss de Cl——g = Sealsfield evidently means Metternich's mistress, Princess Katharina Wilhelmine Friederike of Sagan (1781-1839), a born princess of Courland. Princess Gabriele Auersperg, née Lobkowitz, known at the Congress of Vienna as the "la beauté sentimentale," suffered the attentions of Alexander
Pragmatic Sanction = issued by Emperor Charles VI in 1713 in an attempt to pass Habsburg lands to his daughter Maria Theresa in the event of no male heirs—which, in fact, came to pass, though the War of the Austrian Succession (1840-1848) ultimately had to confirm the Sanction
Prince A——y = Baron Karl Mack von Leiberich (1752-1828) underestimated the mobility of French troops at Ulm (1805) and suffered a tremendous defeat
Prince Kaunitz = Wenzel Anton Kaunitz-Rietberg (1711-1794), chancellor under Maria Theresa, Joseph II, and Francis I
Prince of S——o = Prince of Salerno, Leopold Johann Joseph (1790-1851), married Francis's daughter Maria Klementina in 1816
Prince Schwarzenberg = Prince Karl Philipp zu Schwarzenberg (1771-1820), one of the most successful generals during the Napoleonic Wars, gaining victory at Bar-sur-Aube (1814) and thereby hastening Napoleon's unconditional abdication
Prince Thurn and Taxis, and Count Thun = presumably Prince Maximilian Karl von Thurn and Taxis (1802-1871), and Count Josef Matthias von Thun-Hohenstein (1794-1855), two nobles, pressed into service as actors on this private stage
Professor W——in Berlin = possibly Friedrich August Wolf (1759-1824), a major influence on the founding of the (Humboldt)

university in Berlin

Premysl = earliest dynasty of Bohemia, founded in the 8th century by the legendary peasant Premysl, with St. Wenceslaus ("Good King Wenceslaus") as an early Christian leader

P——ss L——y = Countess Therese Lazansky, born Freiin Bretfeld-Chlumczansky zu Cronenburg

Q——n of his P——n M——y = possibly the Queen of his Prussian Majesty

quadrille = square dance for four couples, consisting of five or six figures

queues = a braid of hair at the back of the head, pigtail

Raphael, Mengs, Skreta, Brändel = the artists Anton Raphael Mengs (1728-1779), Karl Skreta (1604-74), and Peter Johann Brändel (1668-1735)

redemptionaries = immigrants to America who obtained passage by becoming indentured servants

referat = portfolio, responsibility

Regensburg... Aspern... Wagram = Archduke Charles led a war of liberation against Napoleon; the Battle of Regensburg (April 1809) was won by Napoleon, the Battle of Aspern (May 1809) was an Austrian victory, until the Battle of Wagram (July 1809) when the exhausted Austrians were defeated and forced to make major territorial concessions in the Treaty of Schönbrunn in October of that year

restaurateurs = proprietors of restaurants

R——n C——t = Russian court, i.e., Czar Alexander

R——n E——r = the Russian Emperor Alexander I

Robespierre, Napoleon, Charles X = here an allusion to hypocrisy, i.e., executioners during the French Revolution, plunderers during Napoleon's conquests, pious priests following the Wars of Liberation and thus the eventual defeat of France

Rothschild and his brethren = Salomon Mayer Rothschild (1774-1855), the wealthy Viennese banker who supported the Habsburgs; his "brethren," Bernhard von Eskeles (1753-1839) and Leopold von Herz (1767-1828) were co-founders of the Austrian National Bank in 1816

roués = someone devoted to a life of sensual pleasure, a debauchee, rake

Rübezahl, king of the Sudites = Rübezahl, a legendary kindly giant who lived in the Bohemian forests

Russian Autocrat = Czar Alexander I (1777-1825)

sabreure arrogance = the arrogance of a swordsman or cavalry officer

Sand = Karl Ludwig Sand (1759-1820), murdered the writer and Russian statesman August von Kotzebue in 1819

sans gêne = without embarrassment or constraint, freely and easily

Saus and Braus = to live the high life

savans = savants, persons of learning — here: ironic for imbeciles

Schiller's Maria Stuart = classical drama from 1800, exemplifying humanistic values in opposition to ignoble political intrigue, a rough analogy to the relationship between Bohemia and the Austrian Empire at this time

Schönbrunn... St. Stephen = Schönbrunn, palace and Imperial summer residence for the Habsburgs, and St. Stephen's cathedral are landmarks of Vienna to this day

Scythian fetters = an obscure allusion to the political bondage and stifling atmosphere of post-Napoleonic Europe

serviette = table napkin

Seven Years' War = 1756-1763, a worldwide conflict between Austria, France, Russia, Saxony, and Sweden (later Spain) against Prussia, Hanover, and Great Britain; the main result was Prussia's ascendance in power at Austria's expense

Shakespeares, Addisons, and Miltons = William Shakespeare (1564-1616) dramatist and poet, Joseph Addison (1672-1719) essayist and poet, John Milton (1608-1674) poet, here the epitome of English thought and literature

Siam = present-day Kingdom of Thailand, with its capitol at Bangkok

sic tempora mutantur = Thus the times are changed

Slawata and Martinitz = Wilhelm Count Slawata (1572-1652), the chancellor of Bohemia; he and Jaroslav Borita von Martinitz (1582-1649), as representatives of the Emperor, were thrown from the window of the Prague Diet in 1618 by Protestants in the Defenestration of Prague which led to the Thirty Year's War

Sobieskis and Casimirs = John Sobieski, King of Poland (1674-1696) and champion of Polish independence; Casimirs I-IV constituted the Polish royal family and ruled from roughly

1040-1492, uniting and consolidating their territory
sot = stupid, foolish
Spontini's Olympia = successful opera by the Italian composer Gasparo Luigi Pacifico Spontini (1774-1851)
Sprudel = Of more than a dozen active warm springs in Carlsbad, the best-known and hottest, the Sprudel, gushes a geyser of hot water (162° F) to a height of 37 feet
St. John of Nepomuk = the martyred patron saint of Bohemia
St. Paul's Church = a London landmark since the 17th century, thus a standard for the English reader's comparison
table d'hote = a set menu offered to all guests at a fixed price
Te Deums = Christian hymns of praise to God
Temple of Hygæia = thermal baths, long known for their curative and restorative powers
térzettos = music pieces for a trio of musicians
tester = covering or canopy over a bed, or in this case a couch
Teutonic costume = presumably the uniform of a member of *Teutonia*, a student fraternity
T—f— K—z = Metternich's own brother-in-law, the libertine Prince Kaunitz
that privilege = the feudal custom of *droit du seigneur*, the lord's presumptive right to sleep with new brides on their wedding night before their vassal-husbands do; thus the remark about this Elector's many children
The Burghers of Vienna = popular play from 1813 by Adolf Johann Bäuerle (1786-1859)
trammels = shackles, anything impeding progress or development
Tuileries, Palais Royal = since the late 16th century, the Tuileries Palace and its stylized gardens in Paris had been a meeting place for elegant society
turnkey = watchman, guard; one who has charge of the keys in a jail
Tycho Brahe = (1546-1601), Danish astronomer, settled in Prague in 1599 under the patronage of Emperor Rudolf II
underwood = undergrowth, underbrush
Vandamme = Count Dominik Vandamme (1751-1831), French general
vis-à-vis = here, someone across from you, facing you
viva voce = out loud

Vivat! Vivat! = Hurrah! Long live the Queen!

viz = that is to say, namely

"*Voilà des acclamations qui sont sincere*" = "Listen, their cheers are sincere."

Voilà les barbares, les Prussiens, qui ont remportés les chevaux! — Voilà les bêtes des Autriciens! etc. *Voilà les barbares . . .* = Here are the barbarians, the Prussians, who won by the skin of their teeth! — Here are the Austrian beasts!

Waldstein, Schlick, Frangipan = Albrecht Wenzel Eusebius von Waldstein (or Wallenstein, 1583-1634), Count Joachim Andreas Schlick (1569-1621), and Count Franz Christoph Frangipan von Tersat (?-1671) — all were executed for treason

Wallenstein, William Tell = threatening plays by Schiller (performed 1800 and 1804, respectively), due to their revolutionary tone and anti-Austrian sentiment

Wallis = Josef Count Wallis (1767-1818), president of the Imperial treasury

Walter Scott, Moore, and Cowper = the romantic English writer Sir Walter Scott (1771-1832), the Irish romantic poet Thomas Moore (1779-1852), the pre-romantic English poet William Cowper (1731-1800)

weathercock = a weather vane; here, a person who changes readily

Werner's Twenty-eighth (sic) *February* = the dramatist Zacharias Werner (1768-1823) and his most successful play, *The Twenty-Fourth of February*, a highly original, sensational, pioneering Romantic tragedy of fate

whist and ombre parties = whist is a card game for four players, similar to bridge; ombre is a three-handed card game

wicket = a small gate

Wends = a Slavic tribe in northern and eastern Germany

Wittgenstein = Wilhelm Ludwig Georg Count (later Prince) zu Sayn-Wittgenstein (1770-1851), Royal Prussian chamberlain, minister

Zwentibold . . . Arnulf = Arnulf of Carinthia (850?-899), the illegitimate son of Carloman, deposed his uncle, Emperor Charles III the Fat, and became king of Germany, was later crowned Holy Roman Emperor in 896; Zwentibold was Arnulf's own illegitimate son, named by his father as king of the district later called Lorraine